The Mystery of Collective Intelligence

The key to survival in a competitive world

By

George M. White, PhD

The Mystery of Collective Intelligence:
The Key to Survival in a Competitive World

By George M. White, PhD

This book first published 2022

Ethics International Press Ltd, UK

British Library Cataloguing in Publication Data

A catalogue record for this book is available from the British Library

Print Book ISBN: 978-1-871891-31-7

eBook ISBN: 978-1-871891-32-4

Contents

SECTION 1: INTRODUCTION

PREFACE

Collective intelligence is the ability of groups of people to make better decisions than individuals. The degree of intelligence in groups is determined by a variety of factors that can be manipulated by group organizers or sponsors. Without control of these factors, groups are no smarter than individuals; but with them, groups can literally seem possessed of genius. Similarly, there are organizational principles that consistently enhance organizational performance and these principles form the basis of organizational intelligence and long-term survival.

Before we dive into the science behind organizational and collective intelligence, I'd like to share an example of genes that promote the growth of intelligence.

My wife and I once found an abandoned newborn kitten. It was the size of my thumb, hairless, eyes shut, and helpless. So, we found some powdered milk, added water, and with an eyedropper kept the little creature alive. For a while, this required getting up every couple of hours in the night. Eventually the little animal grew into a kitten, all by transforming powdered milk and water into flesh, bones, hair, and everything else that composes an animal.

I couldn't help but marvel at the process whereby genes can transform inanimate stuff such as powdered milk, into a living, breathing animal. It works because the animal's genes set off a series of tissue constructions as the right genes are turned on or off as the animal develops. We now have a beautiful, curious ball of fur with eyes and a fluffy tail that follows us around the house. We became the beneficiaries of the process of genetic learning that took place over millions of years to produce the blueprint for little kittens. The genes that evolved over millions of years produce kittens that can learn in a single lifetime.

The same process is at work in business and governmental organizations today but operating on different timescales. For the past several thousand years, organizational genes in the form of rules, laws, customs, and technical know-how have been evolving to make possible businesses, nations, and the totality of civilization today. And these human organizations actually have a form of intelligence that supports real-time organizational learning. In fact, we will be able to demonstrate later in the book that the more successful organizations are the ones that create platforms for the growth of intelligence, not those focusing on short-term fixes for immediate problems.

Intelligence is the ability of any organization (human organizations or biological life forms) to learn from experience, recognize opportunities and threats, and take action to enhance its chances of survival. This ability has been the guiding force behind evolution on earth beginning 3.5 billion years ago. Learning encoded in biological genes captured the lessons necessary for survival of the first life forms that emerged from the primordial soup. Genes learned to survive through modifying the organizations that carried them. And this process is guiding the evolution of business, government, and the ecosystem of modern civilization.

Before returning to practical issues, I would like to take a few paragraphs to quickly explain the abstract concept of evolution of intelligence in our businesses and governments.

Organizational genes mediate the growth of intelligence in mankind's social organizations. At the level of civilization, we see marvelously complex systems such as satellite communication, the Internet, and global transportation networks working well with no human architect planning the global system. The entire system works as if it were being guided by an intelligent hidden hand.

In fact, "the hidden hand" is the interplay between the constituent parts being built by businesses which are themselves constantly improving because of competitive pressures. Each of these businesses competes based on their organizational intelligence which grows out of their organizational genes. Some companies go out of business and are replaced by others that are more efficient. Over time, *only the more intelligent businesses and nations survive,* and thus over time the intelligence of the ensemble grows larger, and the surviving companies & nations more intelligent.

For example, we will be able to show later in the book that the world's largest companies have superior organizational intelligence based on their superior platforms for discovering knowledge, sharing it and acting on it. We will describe the organizational genes of these companies in chapter 7 (see Walmart, Visa, Microsoft, and other examples).

Let me summarize now by saying, organizational success depends on organizational intelligence derived from organizational genes in the form of rules & regulations & laws & culture & technical knowledge for both businesses and governments. The objective of this book is to explore the practical genes that we might intentionally manipulate to make businesses and governments more intelligent and relevant.

To give a concrete example of the process of evolution in business, and implicitly evolution of organizational genes, consider the process in which new companies with new technologies disrupt established companies. The disrupted companies frequently decline substantially or go out of business altogether—witness the decline of mighty companies: IBM, Sears, JCPenney's, Blockbuster, Kodak, etc. The system of governance in these companies did not allow them to learn fast enough to meet the challenges of disrupting companies. IBM should be what Apple is today (the world's most stock market valued technology company), Sears should be what Walmart is today, Blockbuster should have become Netflix, etc. But the incumbents just didn't see the disruption coming. Their governing genes failed them. <u>It is not simply the emergence of new technology that kills companies. It is a failure of company intelligence</u> to learn, to see what's next, and to adapt.

This book explains, through examples, some of the genes of governance that lead to superior foresight, adaptability, intelligence and therefore survival.

The process of technology innovation and business disruption was brilliantly described by Clayton Christensen in his book, *The Innovator's Dilemma* (1997). He stated that the dilemma faced by most companies is whether to listen to their customers or to their internal innovators. He says most companies listen to their customers (as they are taught to in the best business schools in the country). But customers, it turns out, are not expert at spotting disruptive technology.

Christensen did dig deeper and concluded that it is not sufficient to simply look at technological innovation by itself, you need to look at what competitors are doing with innovation. It is not simply the invention of new technologies that endanger incumbent companies. It is, rather, new technologies serving *new markets at lower costs* in the hands of new companies that allows the new companies to gradually eat into the markets of the incumbents. By the time the incumbents notice, it is too late for them to save themselves.

This raises the question, "Why don't the incumbents defend themselves from smaller competitors with new technologies?" Christensen says incumbents don't notice the encroachment in time because of "the law of resource dependency," which states that corporate resources are always focused on serving existing customers, rather than investigating potential sources of disruption. This is a brilliant insight but is clearly not a sufficient answer. Christiansen himself, with two co-authors, in the book *The Innovator's DNA,* went on to focus on innovation as a partial remedy. They recommend employees and companies practice activities under the general headings of associative thinking, questioning, observing, experimenting, and networking. But, again, there is much more involved.

These things would help companies behave intelligently, but there are many other things that must be considered. For example, crowdsourcing information, deliberative discussions (discussions with psychological safety & balanced turn-taking), sharing financial information inside organizations, procedures promoting innovative activities, diversity, empathy, ethical behavior, respect, and civility in the workplace, having more women in senior positions, minimization of rules and regulations, a culture of valuing people more than numerical outcomes, and the list goes on. All these things part of organizational intelligence as will be explained in detail later in the book.

The objective of this book is to explain some of the many ways of increasing organizational intelligence so that teams, businesses, and governments can be better at serving the needs of humanity.

CHAPTER 1: THE EVOLUTION OF AN INTELLIGENT ISLAND: SINGAPORE

To illustrate the power of good governmental genes, I'd like to share the story of Singapore.

Singapore is a city-state of six million people located on a small island at the tip of Southeast Malaysia. It was a British colony for 144 years until it briefly became a state in Malaysia in 1963. It was kicked out of Malaysia in 1965 when it had a population of 2.5 million. At that time, its per capita income was roughly $500 a year, the same as Ghana. Two-thirds of the country lived in slums. It was a small jungle island with a small seaport, a seemingly inconsequential "dot" at the tip of Malaysia in the 1960s.

Today Singapore is now one of the most prosperous countries in the world. Its GDP per capita ranks Singapore seventh in the world as of 2020 (theglobaleconomy, 2020). They have more millionaires per capita than any other nation on the planet, except possibly for oil-rich kingdoms in the Middle East. For the past several years, Singapore has been among the top-ranked countries in the world for ease of doing business, competitiveness, and lack of corruption. Singapore has the world's fastest peak internet speeds, possibly the world's most remarkable botanical garden, and certainly the world's most beautiful airport. The city is practically crime-free, with large swaths of jungle green still visible in the heart of town.

Singapore's successes have been achieved without oil or other natural resources. Its main resource has been the intelligence of its government operating within the framework provided by its governmental DNA.

While working in Singapore a few years ago, I would sometimes fly over the jungles of Malaysia and look down on patches where the jungle had given way to small settlements. The farmers and fishermen below were toiling away as they had for centuries. As we approached the island of Singapore, however, glittering skyscrapers sprang up from the jungle. I was always filled with awe for the same reason that I marveled at my kitten-turned-cat.

I was in awe of the miracle of governmental DNA that could transform the jungle into such a marvelous city in one generation. The miracle was highlighted by the fact that the neighboring country had all the same raw materials but remained rural.

Exactly what were the organizational genes that allowed Singapore to transform the jungle to a wealthy Metropolis when neighboring peoples are still plowing behind oxen (symbolically speaking)?

At its inception on August 9, 1965, the Republic of Singapore had been a British colony for more than a century. Thus, they had the opportunity to start their nation with governmental genes from Great Britain, a multiparty parliamentary democracy that had been evolving and improving for centuries. To these genes, the country founders added their own unique embellishments over several decades to create a uniquely successful form of government.

Singapore's founding prime minister, Lee Kuan Yew was a young Chinese idealist educated in British law, who thought of himself as a socialist more than a capitalist. As a result, he married socialistic ideas with the better parts of democracy practiced in Great Britain. What evolved over the years is a hybrid between socialism and democracy; a system that has been dominated by one party, the People's Action Party, for 62 years. In addition, the dominant force in the PAP has been Lee Kuan Yew and his family. So, the usual mechanics of democracies have been traded for more of a bureaucratic meritocracy. However, the details are beyond the scope of this chapter.

There may be several organizational genes here but certainly the key gene in Singapore's DNA was Lee Kuan Yew's constant advocacy of acquiring industry and knowledge from more industrialized nations, and his drive to create an infrastructure free of corruption to make Singapore an ideal location for doing business. Another gene may be his drive to create and/or support businesses delivering services useful to the national infrastructure (water, electricity, transportation, communication, banking, law enforcement…to name a few). (A longer list is provided in Chapter 9, Section 6.)

These activities (acquiring knowledge and building infrastructure) increased Singapore's organizational intelligence. These activities always increase the collective intelligence of businesses, as well as nations, and lead to economic success for businesses as well.

Singapore's extraordinary success showcases the *power of good organizational genes (good principles) and the economic success that emerges from their use.*

This example does not pretend to reveal many of the details of how good genes produce intelligence and economic success. That is the subject of the upcoming chapters.

At this point, we need to transition to the power of collective *intelligence,* and see how organizational intelligence benefits from it.

CHAPTER 2: COLLECTIVE INTELLIGENCE

Collective intelligence is the ability of groups of people to make better decisions than individuals can make acting alone. When done right, group decisions can be substantially better than the decisions made by individuals. It is as if the groups exhibit a kind of super intelligence. Furthermore, the apparent learning inside decision-making groups can grow faster than individual learning. These things apply not only in narrow areas, but across the board with regard to such things as innovation, creativity, negotiating, word-completion problems, spatial puzzles, estimation problems, and guiding companies. (See Malone, 2018, 31)

I personally am excited with the possibility that I might use some of these techniques in my own personal decision-making. Knowing that it might be possible to tap into a form of intelligence that exceeds individual human intelligence is truly exciting.

We will see in Chapter 4 that the world's largest and most successful businesses have superior platforms for collective intelligence. As an example, the world's two largest companies (Walmart: based on number of employees, and Visa International: based on the dollar volume of total transactions) both developed superior platforms for utilizing collective intelligence, and it is probable that their successes are a consequence of doing so. Of course, there was no theory of organizational or collective intelligence to guide them when these companies were founded in 1963 and 1970 respectively. Nonetheless, their visionary founders intuitively understood the benefits of organizational flatness, information gathering activities, and organizational learning which are the building blocks of organizational collective intelligence.

It must be understood that collective intelligence, as we use it here, is not an adjective for polling the opinions of groups of people making decisions based on such polling. Much more is involved. It includes guidelines for forming groups, gathering information, analyzing it, discussing it, and ultimately making decisions. These guidelines are not obvious and can take on many forms as will be explored in the rest of the book.

We start with a somewhat famous example of collective intelligence; the "desert survival test", which is typically given to groups of students or trainees in programs to convince them of the powers of group decision-making.

2.1 The Desert Survival Test

I first encountered the "desert survival test" at the Stanford Graduate School of Business. This game is played by Stanford MBA students to teach them the value of teams and is apparently a very popular teaching tool used in many colleges and training programs. NASA has a version where participants assume they have crashed on the moon. But the standard version has people crash landing in the middle of Australia, or the Mojave Desert in California.

Within the test, the instructor says: Suppose you are a survivor of the plane crash in the desert. On the wreckage of the plane, you find these 15 artifacts: flashlight, penknife, map of the area, plastic raincoat, magnetic compass, first aid kit, 45 caliber loaded pistol, parachute (red and white), two bottles of salt tablets, one quart of water per person, a book entitled *Edible Animals of the Desert*, one pair of sunglasses per person, two quarts of vodka, one topcoat per person, and a cosmetic mirror (see Appendix 02).

The students, working alone, create a rank-ordered list of these artifacts, showing the most important artifacts for their survival at the top, and items of lesser importance in descending order. The students then hand in their lists for scoring. After all the students have turned in their list, the class is divided into teams with, typically, four or five students per team. Each team discusses the issues, and then creates their own rank-ordered list of the artifacts. The teams then hand in their ordered lists. After a brief time, the professor and his TAs would evaluate every submission (using a standardized scoring system provided by the developers of the test, as described in the Appendix 02), and then display the scores with the names of the submitting individuals and teams ranked. It soon becomes apparent that team names are at the top; ahead of the names of individuals. Rarely does an individual outperform his team. This drives home the observation that a group is almost always smarter than the smartest person in a group.

If you're wondering how the scoring can be so reliable, check out the Appendix which has an example of how experts attach numerical scores to the questions.

2.2 Diversity in Stanford Design Teams

Diversity of team membership also increases individual team's performances as was demonstrated by Professor Larry Leifer, Founder and Director of the Center for Design Research at Stanford University. Starting in the mid-1980s, Professor Leifer offered a course in engineering design in which students would sign up in the fall and work on designs over a couple of quarters. The designs were for complex systems such as robots, missile nose cones, boats, and so on. There were typically 40 students in the class, and they would n be divided into ten teams; four students per team. When the course was initially offered, and for several years thereafter, team formation was left up to the students. Each team would work on a single design which would be submitted to a national design competition at the end of the second quarter.

The competition was a national design competition organized by the Arc Welders Association of America held in Dearborn, Michigan. Designs were submitted from many universities across America as well as from industry. Up until 1991, Stanford would often have one or two of its teams among the top ten winners of the competition. Then, in 1991, Larry Leifer decided to intervene in the team formation process. Larry decided to assign team members based on diversity. He gave all the students a Minnesota Multiphasic Personality Profile test and also looked at academic majors, age, race, gender, and locations of students' homes. Having done so he then ensured that each team had a variety of different personality types; assigning team membership to maximize diversity.

The effect was dramatic. After 1991, the Stanford teams began placing several of its teams among the top ten in the national competition and won first place for several years. But what was even more dramatic was the fact that Leifer discovered that he could predict the winners (or at least the rank ordering of the teams) after only one or two months into the eight-month course. He did so by counting the number of unique noun phrases in the students' design documents and discussion notes. The larger the number of unique noun phrases, the more likely the team was to win (or rank higher than other teams).

The explanation for this is that noun phrases (a noun preceded by an adjective) are concept markers. So, having more noun phrases meant there were more unique concepts under discussion. It follows that the team with more unique noun phrases in their first month of being together was demonstrating that it was better at collecting or generating concepts for consideration. This, in turn, translated into a higher probability of winning in the competition that followed. It's not exactly clear why greater diversity of team membership allowed teams to have a larger number of concepts. However, it seems likely that diversity of age, academic major, personality type, and so on brought diversity of mental models, and having a larger number of mental models to consider is likely to result in superior designs.

David Kelley, who founded the design company IDEO in 1991, was a colleague and a participant in Larry Leifer's class. Kelley took advantage of Leifer's findings about the diversity of membership in teams and infused it into the culture of IDEO. IDEO went on to become the world's most celebrated design firm, receiving more accolades and media recognition than any other design firm in the world. Diversity was probably the key element in its success. If you ask David Kelly or the senior executives at IDEO about the secret of their success, they will generally say it's "empathy" for the people using the products of their design. By that they mean that designers should put themselves in the shoes of their customers, and constantly keep in mind how customers will use their products.

But there are other cultural genes that promote information sharing and openness in addition to empathy and diversity. Another came straight from the CEO who stated that everyone's goal should be to share and help someone else, rather than aim for accolades personally. IDEO's success has been a primary force behind the current popularity of "Design Thinking." I've attempted to summarize the key elements of Design Thinking from reviews of articles about the IDEO culture. The organization should be characterized by:

1. a flat power structure, i.e., equality among employees
2. extensive employee autonomy (minimal rules and regulations)
3. employees understanding that "your goal is to help others succeed"
4. frequent building and testing of prototypes
5. continual celebration of the spirit of collaboration and information sharing
6. diversity in hiring practices

Doing these things will improve the organizational intelligence of any company by promoting information discovery, information exchange, and discussion. It should be intuitively clear that intelligence thrives on information discovery and exchange. It's not so obvious that discussion is also key. Indeed, it turns out to be absolutely key, as the next section shows.

2.3 Principles of Collective Intelligence

Ray Dalio is the founder, chair, and co-chief investment officer of Bridgewater Associates, probably the most successful hedge fund on earth, with more than $15 billion under management. He uses collective intelligence to manage money, as he explains his TED Talk in April 2017 entitled *"How to build a company where the best ideas win."* In his talk, he said:

> "Collective decision-making is so much better than individual decision-making if it's done well. It's been the secret sauce behind our success. It's why we made more money for our clients than any other hedge fund in existence and made money out of 23 of the last 26 years."

Managing money in the financial markets is fiercely competitive and populated by extremely bright individuals. Hedge funds can afford to hire the best and brightest from MIT, Harvard, and Stanford where they are traditionally given individual responsibilities for managing money. Demonstrating that collective intelligence is superior to the best and the brightest individual decision-makers is quite remarkable and showcases the power of collective intelligence.

There are two broad categories of collective intelligence: active and passive. In the passive form, people are simply asked for their opinions. Individual opinions are then combined with other opinions through voting, idea markets, or smart filtering. Such "Crowdsourcing" or "wisdom of crowds" are examples of "passive" intelligence.

In contrast, in active collective intelligence, discussion and mutual education takes place. Active intelligence is inherently superior to passive intelligence. Of course, when large numbers of people are involved and discussion is impractical, hybrid active/passive systems would be superior to active alone. The *passive* form of collective intelligence was first demonstrated by John Galton, in 1906. He invited 787 members of a crowd to wager a guess as to the weight of an ox and offered a small reward for the closest guess. Apparently, the average of all 787 wagers was 1197 pounds and the actual weight was 1198 pounds. No single individual made a guess as accurate as the collective had guessed.

Numerical averaging is one way, but only one way, of combining individual judgments. A variety of other ways of averaging the opinions of crowds were described James Surowiecki's book, *Wisdom of Crowds: Why the Many Are Smarter Than the Few and How Collective Wisdom Shapes Business,*

Economies, Societies and Nations (2004). Surowiecki's examples demonstrate how averaging opinions, especially when using a "robust average"[1], is significantly better than the estimate/opinion of single individuals.

However, we can do significantly better than simply crowdsourcing when group discussions take place, which is what we call *active* collective intelligence. The power of group discussion was explained nicely in a TED Talk by Mariano Sigman and Dan Ariely entitled *"How Can Groups Make Good Decisions?"* (TED Studio, April 2017). Ariely and Sigman orchestrated a TEDx event in Buenos Aires, Argentina with 10,000 attendees. They asked the attendees to make individual estimates of things such as the height of the Eiffel Tower without discussion. Each person wrote down their answers on a sheet of paper. They then divided the crowd into teams of five and asked them to come up with group answers. The result was that averaging the group answers after they reached consensus was much more accurate than averaging the answers of everyone before debate. In other words, decisions after deliberation are almost always superior to group decisions when people do not deliberate (discuss issues).

We can still do better than simply encouraging discussion by applying better techniques for extracting group opinions. A better decision than a yes-no vote can be reached by allowing different weights to people's opinions, and by allowing voters to attach different weights to their opinions. Ray Dalio, TEDTalk 2017 "How to build a company where the best ideas win", devised a system that he called the "dot collector" which runs on PC laptops or tablets. The dot collector allows discussants to rate whoever is speaking in real time. The system combines everyone's opinions of speakers at the end of the discussion to create a ranking of speakers and, indirectly, the ideas they promoted.

Another more general approach is the "idea market" (Koen, 2014, is recommended for further information). An idea market can take many forms, but the basic idea is to operate a trading market, like the stock market, in which stock is replaced with ideas. Ideas can be outcomes, predictions, preferences, or any statement that does not have a known answer. Everyone in the group is given real or imaginary money to invest in the market. They are told to invest their money in the ideas that they like the most or think that others will like the most as that will drive up the value of popular ideas. What happens next varies widely in terms of the duration of the market, the amounts that can be invested, how profits from trading are distributed (if at all), and discussions between participants.

---

[1]A "robust average" throws out outliers before taking the average.

The idea market has been tried by several major corporations including Google and Hewlett-Packard. They claim that the system predicted sales three months in advance, with only a 10% error (Koen, 2014, 24).

2.4 IQ Test for Collective Intelligence, CI

The possibility that collective intelligence exists in groups was explored rigorously by Anita Woolley at CMU in collaboration with Tom Malone at MIT. They asked: Is it possible that some groups consistently outperform other groups over a range of problems? If so, the concept of there being a collective intelligence of a group would make sense and the collective intelligence (CI) of the group would be measurable.

Given this, they set about devising an intelligence test for groups. They chose a strategy proposed by Joseph McGrath (2018) in which he tested different people's skills in four different task domains: generating, choosing, negotiating, and executing tasks. According to Tom Malone in his book *Superminds* the tasks went as follows:

1. "For tasks involving generating something new, for instance, we asked groups to brainstorm various uses for a brick" (2018, 31).
2. "For tasks involving choosing from among specified alternatives, we asked groups to solve visual puzzles from a standard individual intelligence test called Raven's Matrices" (2018, 31).
3. "For negotiating tasks, we asked members of groups to pretend that they all lived in the same house and then to plan a shopping trip subject to various constraints on travel time, costs, and perishability of the items they needed to buy" (2018, 31).
4. "Finally, for executing tasks, we asked them to type a long text passage into a shared online text-editing system. We also asked them to perform other tasks like word-completion problems, spatial puzzles, and estimation problems" (2018, 31).

The subjects of the study came from the communities around CMU and MIT and were representative of the population of the general US. There was a total of 699 people in 192 groups which were each composed of between two and five people. The key results of subjecting these groups to the tests above showed that CI did in fact exist. Some groups were consistently smarter than other groups across all tests that were thrown at them.

Most importantly, groups were always smarter than the smartest person in the group, in high CI groups. Furthermore, group empathy was a better predictor of performance than the highest IQ in the team as well as the average IQ of the team members.

Having proven that CI exists, Malone and Woolley set out to understand what makes a smart team smart and how might it be possible to make a team smarter? They found that

1. Equal turn-taking in discussions helped.
2. Increasing the number of women on the team helped.
   a. But they also found that having women on teams helps only as long as there is more than one woman on the team and less than 100% of the team is composed of women.
   b. Social perceptiveness or empathy was exceedingly helpful.
3. IQs of team members are not nearly as important as empathy and social perceptiveness. Having a team of smart people isn't as effective as having a team of socially sensitive people (Woolley, 2013).

Empathy (social perceptiveness) was measured by having subjects guess the emotional state of people simply by looking at their eyes with the rest of their faces covered.

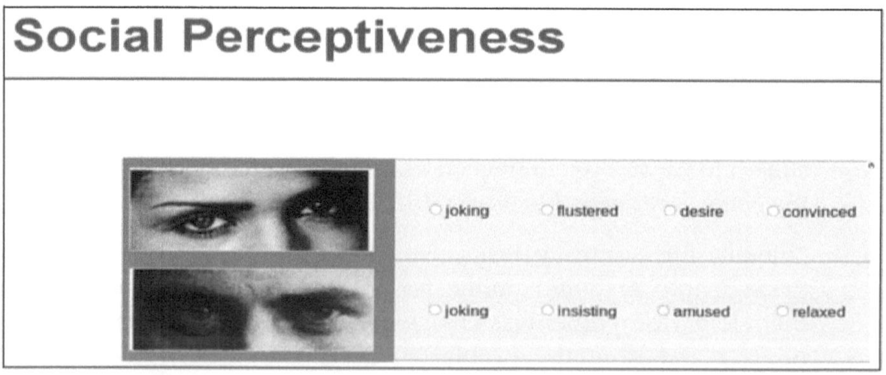

Figure 1: *Social Perceptiveness Test*

Women are better at social perceptiveness than men and this may account for the fact that teams with women do slightly better.

Source: ***Malone, 2018, 34***

The most striking result was that having more women on a team makes the team smarter. This shows up in a very practical sense in the management of corporations. You can see from Graph 01 that having more women in senior management makes companies more profitable. It is hard to ignore such a striking finding. Graph 02 demonstrates the same thing with different data.

Figure 2: ***Cumulative Return on Fortune 1000 Women Led Companies***

According to March 3, 2015, Fortune magazine, Boston-based Quantopian did the study and produced the graph above showing that women-led companies outperform the S&P 500.

Source: ***Fortune Magazine, 2015***

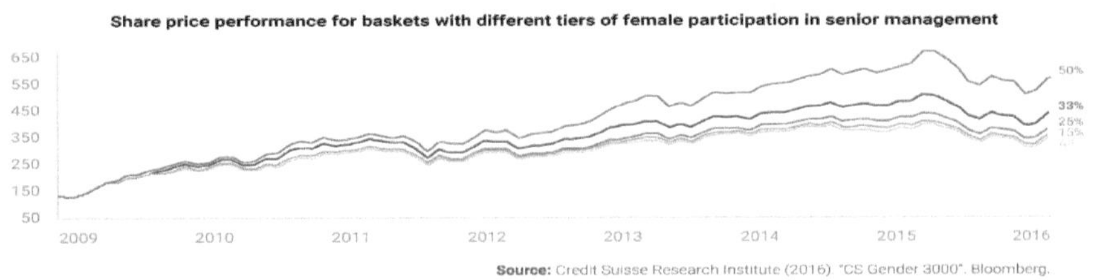

Figure 3: *Share Price for Baskets with Different Tiers of Female Participation in Senior Management*

According to: The Gender 3000 report series, published by the Credit Suisse Research Institute, which provides information on gender diversity within 3,000 companies globally.

Source: ***CSRI, 2016, 25***

Alex Pentland, quoted extensively in Section 2.7, in discussing the productivity of a group in a company, said "The pattern of idea flow by itself was more important to group performance than all other factors and, in fact, was as important as all other factors taken together. Think about it: Individual intelligence, personality, skill, and everything else together mattered less than the pattern of idea flow" (Pentland, 2014, 85). Alex was referring to flow of communication which resulted in equal involvement of everyone in the group/company with a vested interest. This is another way of saying that everyone in a company needs to be more or less equally engaged in discussing issues that require decisions which impact strategic planning or resource allocation. It follows that organizational intelligence benefits from having as many brains as possible involved in decision-making.

2.5 The Mysterious Power of Empathy in Group Decision-Making

It has been shown that having empathetic team members helps teams to make better decisions. Why should this be true? The initial answers are surprising and only deepen the mystery.

Researchers at MIT and CMU conjectured that empathetic people are better able to read social signals, and this would promote efficient problem-solving dialogues. To test this hypothesis, research carried out under the direction of Tom Malone and Anita Woolley (2018) investigated group behavior when group members could neither see nor hear each other. They were forced to communicate through typed messages. The results were the same. It follows that body language or other typical nonverbal cues were not the mechanisms whereby empathy between team members was having its effect.

The answer must be more subtle. Perhaps it has to do with intuition and subconscious thinking?

The right and left hemispheres of the human brain have substantially different functions. The left hemisphere houses our linguistic skills and our consciousness. It stores memories as decomposable units which are recombined to form the memories that we are conscious of. The right hemisphere, on the other hand, has no language and is very fast to recognize things; an order of magnitude faster than the left hemisphere. Because it is responsible for vigilance, it has to be fast. The right hemisphere does not use logic but rather associations as its fundamental mental process.

Curiously, the right hemisphere may be more "intelligent" because it tends to produce more "aha" insights, as has been shown by fMRI brain monitoring of people solving hard problems. It is the location of our intuitions, and by some criteria, the location of our deeper insights. The "fast and slow thinking" that takes place in the two hemispheres may shed light on group intelligence (Kahneman, 2011). Smart people are traditionally judged to be smart, i.e., judged to have higher IQs, because they are good at using the skills of their left hemisphere, the slow thinking side. When you give an individual human being a problem to solve, they start out using their left hemisphere. This works fine if the problem is of the sort we are taught to solve in schools. But on really novel hard problems, logical thinking appears to be inferior to intuitive thinking which involves the right hemisphere; the seat of intuition.

Does group discussion help members access the intuition of the right hemisphere? Consider that having empathetic people on teams improves performance. Empathy originates primarily in the right hemisphere, that part of the brain in charge of recognizing danger, friend / foe, and body language.

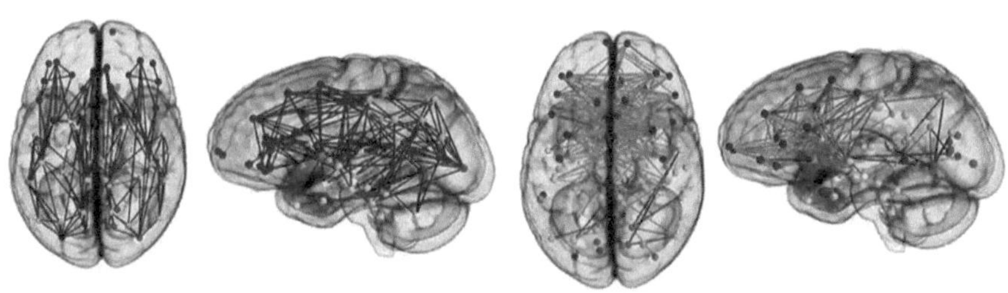

Neural map of a typical man's brain. Photograph: National Academy of Sciences/PA

Neural map of a typical woman's brain. Photograph: National Academy of Sciences/PA

Figure 4: *The Male Brain and the Female Brain*

Neural activity is highest in nerves that stay within one hemisphere in men, in contrast to nerves that crossover shown on the right which characterize women's brains.

Source: ***National Academy of Sciences, 2013***

In addition, the more women on teams, the better the team performance. And women are known to be more empathetic than men. Furthermore, women also have larger corpora callosa, the nerve bundles connecting the two hemispheres, when compared to men.

Some studies have shown that neural activity in men tends to stay in one hemisphere rather than cross over and involve the other hemisphere. The neural activity in women's brains, on the other hand, crosses over between the two hemispheres frequently. One of the reasons that group intelligence can be superior to the sum of individual intelligences may arise from people in groups making better use of their right hemispheres. We do not know how to communicate directly with the right hemisphere, but we do know from fMRI experiments that there is frequently a burst of activity in the right hemisphere when a person has an "aha" moment. When we solve our hardest problems, the answers seem to come from the right hemisphere. When groups demonstrate superior intelligence to individuals, it may be because the group has tapped into the right hemisphere intuition of its individual members.

A different reason that thinking in groups may have superior outcomes is revealed by Stephen Sloman, Brown University and Philip Fernbach, University of Colorado. They point out that an individual's memory depends on people and things around them (Cook, 2017). Memory is actually a combination of search strategies and stored information. In other words, when we are asked to explain anything, we can all start off by recalling all the details that we can remember. However, there will come a boundary at which our individual knowledge becomes insufficient, and we have to get missing information from an external source. We do not think alone, i.e., we rely on our mate, the internet, notes, books, Google, and the physical world to provide that information which we do not carry in our heads. This is where search strategy comes into play, knowing where to look. If it is the nature of thought to have external memory cues and knowledge sources, it's easy to understand that if you are in a group, you will find other people who can help you elaborate something at the boundary of your personal knowledge. So, you may actually become more intelligent, in a narrow domain, as a consequence of discussing matters with a group.

2.6 Social and Emotional Intelligence and Team Success

Professor Alex Pentland, and his graduate students at MIT, explored the question: can rules of conduct make teams smarter? Alex Pentland is one of the most cited and celebrated authors in computer science in the world. He is also a member of the Institute for Collective Intelligence at MIT, headed by Tom Malone.

In their work, Pentland and his students looked at multiple industries as well as individuals working inside and outside of teams. They looked at "innovation teams, post-op wards in hospitals, customer-facing teams in banks, backroom operations teams, and call center teams" (2014, 219). The research was carried out by having people wear electronic sociometric badges that measured tone of voice, body language, and who talked to whom, without actually monitoring any of the words spoken.

The research showed that how people spoke to one another in meetings, independently of the words spoken, was a *better predictor of team success* than individual intelligence, personality, skill, and/or specialized knowledge. In fact, Pentland and his team were able to predict which teams would win in business plan competitions or make more money in financial investment negotiations based solely on the tone of voice and the evidence of enthusiastic cooperation, without ever hearing the actual words spoken.

Pentland (2014) also looked at balanced communications versus unbalanced communications and was able to show that the more equal contributions were, the better a team performed. This is exactly what Anita Woolley also found, as mentioned in Chapter 2.

Pentland (2014) also confirmed Anita Woolley's (2013) result that the IQ of participants is not a strong predictor of success. But empathy is. This is striking because human linguistic skills reside in the left hemisphere of the human brain, whereas nonverbal cues which define how you talk to someone reside in the right hemisphere. Could the power of collective intelligence come from right hemispheric thinking?

Putting aside the neurological basis for behavior, it is certain that nonverbal and nonlogical behaviors end up influencing group intelligence. Pentland (2014) thinks that the productivity of groups is determined by the energy, exploration, and engagement of team members. At the same time, enthusiasm and energy are social motivators. Exploration of new facts not known to the group always helps educate the group eventually. And finally, honest interest and commitment of people shows up in engagement and helps everyone remain motivated.

Coyle (2018) mentioned in his book, *The Culture Code,* that Pentland suggests that the following rules of conduct increased team performance:

1. "Everyone on the team must talk and listen in roughly equal measure and keep contributions short and sweet.
2. Members should face one another, and their conversations and gestures should be energetic.
3. Members should connect directly with one another—not just with the team leader.
4. Members should carry on back-channel or side conversations within the team.
5. Members should periodically break, go exploring outside the team, and bring information back" (2018, 14 - 15).

Pentland also gave a profound insight into the nature of idea exchanges: The characteristics typical of the highest-performing groups included:

1. "a larger number of ideas: many short statements rather than a few long ones;

2. dense interactions: a lot of quick statements and rebuttals that serve to encourage contributions and build consensus;
3. diversity of ideas: everyone speaking up with good turn taking among the participants" (2014, 85)

What is striking about the work of Pentland, is their connection to the findings of Larry Leifer at Stanford in his design classes as noted in Chapter 2. Leifer discovered that the larger the number of unique noun phrases used in design discussions the more likely a team was to win the eight-month long design competition. Prof Leifer also discovered that diversity in team membership was helpful.

2.7 Balancing Communication in Organizations

Communication patterns in companies were studied by Pentland (2014). It was found that after management was encouraged to mandate more balanced communication, company productivity picked up in the areas studied.

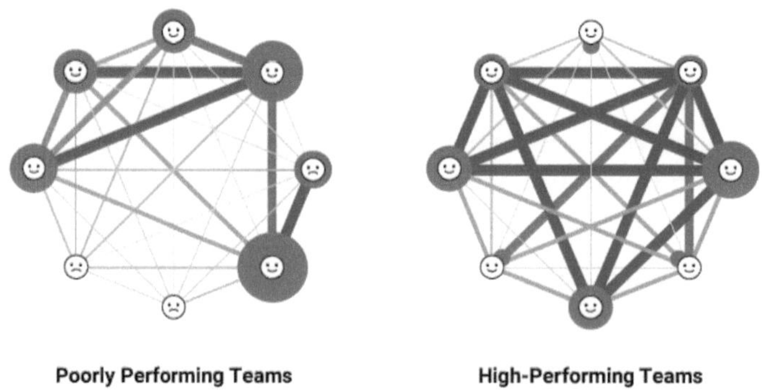

Figure 5: *Frequency of Communication Between Team Members*

This diagram implies that company division success is correlated with how uniformly people communicate among team members -- in a poorly performing division versus a high-performing division.

Source: ***Pentland, 2012***

Pentland noted, referring to the productivity of a company group: "what these sociometric data showed was that the pattern of idea flow by itself was more important to group performance than all other factors and, in fact, was as important as all other factors taken together. Think about it: Individual intelligence, personality, skill, and everything else together mattered less than the pattern of idea flow" (2014, 85). This is one of the strongest statements I can imagine and implies that collective intelligence is superior to individual intelligence. In addition, it also suggests how to access it, namely, through a balanced idea flow between everyone in a team.

2.8 The collision of ideas and the benefits thereof

Would you imagine that your wealth, health, and longevity could be influenced by the diversity in your social contacts, or the diversity in the neighborhood you live in, or the nation in which you live?

According to Pentland (2014), this is indeed the case. Pentland was able to show that exposure to different ideas - the collision of ideas you are immersed in - is how, on average, you as an individual can increase your success in life. One way of being exposed to different ideas is to live in a culturally diverse community or country.

In 2012, Nature magazine described a hundred odd page research paper by Oded Galor of Brown University and Quamrul Ashraf of Williams College in Williamstown, Massachusetts which summarized research covering 145 Countries looking at *genetic diversity and per capita income* (Callaway, 2012).

The paper by Galor and Ashraf showed that genetically diverse nations possessed greater rates of innovation and generally produced better economic outcomes.

Why diversity might matter was explored by Rock and Grant for HBR (2016) in their paper, by "Why Diverse Teams Are Smarter." The article covered work by Pentland (2014) who had been able to persuade various phone companies and credit card companies to let him (and his various students at MIT) analyze credit card transactions and the locations of phones and mobile phones, (after personally identifiable information was removed). The data showed that the greater diversity in the people that you talk to, the more improvement in your economic standing (increased longevity, wealth, health, and general well-being).

In one such study conducted by Pentland in the UK, telecommunications data was collected during the month of August 2005. The data collected covered more than 90% of the mobile phones in the country, and more than 99% of residential and business landlines. Data was accessed in the UK government's Index of Multiple Deprivation which provides a composite measure of the prosperity of 32,482 communities (Crown, 2007). It includes data on income, employment, education, health, crime, housing, and environmental quality. The data does not identify individuals, but it did allow Pentland's researchers to correlate individual prosperity with measurements of who called whom for one month. The data showed that the wealth and prosperity of individual people is proportional to the amount of exposure that they have to other people who would be considered "diverse"; those that lived further away, were within a different economic enclave, or possessed a different socioeconomic status.

Is important to note that this correlation may not be causal but, rather, consequential. In other words, poor people may simply not have diverse connections. On the other hand, it may be that having diverse connections does create prosperity. I suspect that it does. Pentland (2018) was also able to show that diversity of social contacts was, on average, even more important to an individual's success than education. In other words, diversity in a person's social network was even more important than the person's education. This hypothesis "worked not only for people individually, but for entire communities. As people in any particular community interact with other communities, the average income for the community increases in proportion to the diversity of communication between the communities. (Data were taken from 100,000 randomly chosen people in a mid-income country.)" (Pentland, 2018)

Pentland goes on to say "Wealth comes from finding new opportunities. Long-term economic growth is primarily driven by innovation, and those cities that facilitate human interaction and idea exchange needed for good ideas and new opportunities are the most innovative" (2018, 5).

Pentland continued: "We found that *if* a city's infrastructure facilitates more diverse physical interactions, *then* over the long term, the citizens make more money. [...] So, if you want to make a richer city, make its transportation system better," says Pentland (2018, 4) (in other words, make it possible to easily travel to and mingle with people in diverse ghettos, enclaves, districts, and/or socially distinct parts of town). This model also predicts GDP per square kilometer extremely accurately, in both the US and EU. What this suggests, according to Pentland, is that the factors that we usually think about—investment, education, infrastructure, institutions—may not be the direct causes of GDP growth. Instead, the main drivers of progress in society may be social interactions and, implicitly, the search for new opportunities rather than people's skills or capital investment.

2.9 Richard Florida: The Power of Regional Diversity

Richard Florida developed a metric which would predict that Silicon Valley would emerge where it did based on diversity and quality of life offered there. He did this by studying diversity in different regions and he found that diversity increases innovation and economic output. He then developed a quantitative measure of these things and it turned out that Silicon Valley was at the top of the ranking.

His first book, *The Rise of the Creative Class,* started out by showing that knowledge workers who have the luxury of deciding where they would like to work will choose the geographical areas that have a better quality of life and more diversity. These tend to be locations that maximize the number of lifestyle options for residents. This always means a metropolitan area with a large variety of cultures, entertainment, and recreational facilities and the smallest number of social stigmas attached to a person's choices or ethnicity or gender or sexuality or country of origin.

So, Florida invented various indices to measure the cultural diversity offered in a region. He produced a composite diversity index, which confirms that the most innovative regions in the country have the greatest diversity, as we can see by looking at the index in Figure 6.

It's remarkable that this Table predicts Silicon Valley should happen where it did, in the shadow of San Francisco, which tops the list for diversity and liberal thinking.

In an article published in 2002 by the Brookings Institute, Prof. Florida states:

Social, cultural, and ethnic diversity are strong indicators of a metropolitan area's high-technology success. Our argument about diversity is simple and straightforward. Diversity of human capital is a key component of the ability to attract and retain a high technology industry. To demonstrate this, we constructed a Composite Diversity Index (CDI) measure based on the three diversity indicators that we discussed earlier—the gay and bohemian indices and the percent of foreign-born residents. We ranked our 50 metropolitan areas by each indicator (low to high) and summed the three rankings. The CDI strongly correlates with the Milken Tech-Pole Ranking (2002).

Diverstity Ranking by Metropolitian Area

Milken Tech-Pole Ranking	Metropolitan Area	Composite Diversity Ranking
1	San Francisco	2
2	Boston	6
3	Seattle	5
4	Washington D.C	3
5	Dallas	15
6	Los Angeles	1
7	Chicago	11
8	Atlanta	14
9	Phoenix	21
10	New York	4
11	Philadelphia	32
12	San Diego	7
13	Denver	17
14	Austin	8
15	Houston	18

Source: Florida, R. (2002). The Rise of the Creative Class

Figure 6: *Diversity Ranking by Metropolitan Area*

Source: **Florida, R. (2002)**

As Figure 6 demonstrates, the top 11 metro areas on the CDI are also among the top 15 Milken Tech-Pole regions. This offers strong evidence as to the importance of the combined effects of social, cultural, and "ethnic diversity for both high-tech location and growth" (Florida, 2002). In other words, Florida concludes that diversity is good for businesses and innovation. It can be concluded that diversity increases organizational intelligence.

CHAPTER 3: THOUGHT LEADERS ON ORGANIZATIONAL GENES FOR INNOVATION

The following are experts in creating and leading highly innovative teams. They do not ascribe their advice to collective intelligence. However, the techniques they describe actually promote what we would call collective intelligence.

3.1 Rocio Lorenzo: The Power of Women in Companies

An endorsement for *diversity* in decision-making teams comes from Rocio Lorenzo who gave a TED Talk in Milan, Italy in 2017, entitled "How diversity makes teams more innovative". Rocio reported on a study carried out with the Technical University of Munich involving 171 companies in Germany, Austria, and Switzerland. The study asked companies two things: how innovative they are, and how diverse they are. For innovation, companies were asked how much revenue was generated from new products or services. For diversity, companies were asked about the gender, nationality, industry, career, age, and education of employees.

The results obtained were unequivocal. "More diverse companies are simply more innovative, period," (Lorenzo, 2017). She went on to say that, of the 100 largest publicly listed companies in Germany, only 30 had a woman (one woman) on their board, and that 100% of these companies had male CEOs. This shows just how suboptimal strategic management is in German companies.

Lorenzo's team also looked at the participation of women in senior management and found that if a company had more than 20% female participation, there was a significant increase in innovation revenue going from 15% to 25%. Consistent with the studies done by Anita Woolley (2013) that we covered earlier in Chapter 2, if companies had fewer than 20% participation by women, they had no increase in revenue. In other words, one woman can get talked down by all-male team members. But having two or more women on the team is likely to increase creativity and innovation.

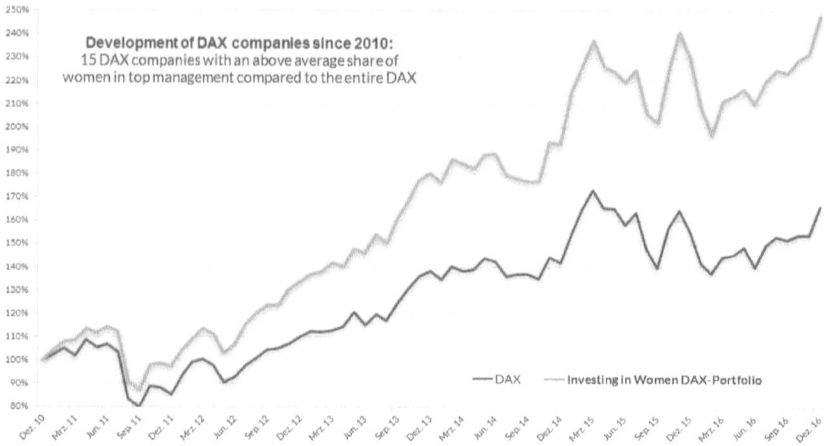

Figure 7: *Development of DAX Companies since 2010*

Investing in women in management 15 DAX companies

Source: ***investing-in-women.com, 2016***

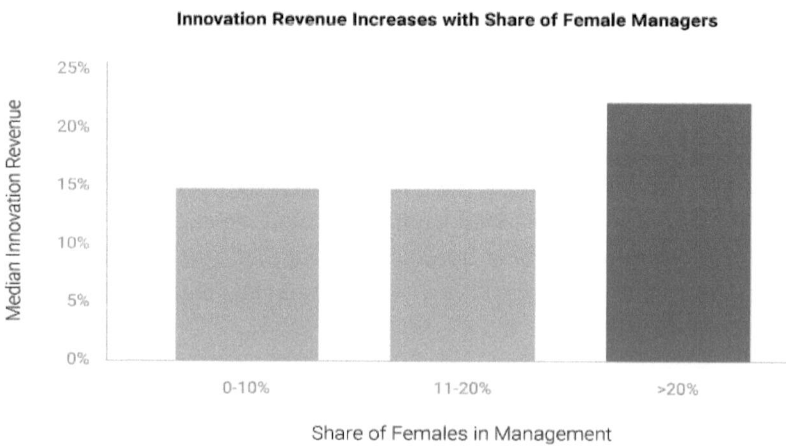

Figure 8: *Innovation Revenue Increases with Share of Female Managers*

Source: ***Lorenzo (2016)***

In 2019 Credit Suisse looked at 3,000 firms from around the world and showed that companies with more female senior management had higher levels of profitability as well. In another study conducted by S&P Global, published in October 2019, share prices between 2000 and 2019 looked at "gender diversity." The study followed share price changes for 5,825 new executive appointments. It was found that for the two years following the appointment of a woman CEO, there was a 20% improvement in share price compared to male CEO appointments.

All this provides more evidence that women are better at exploiting the collective intelligence in their organizations. This is consistent with our understanding of intelligence; namely, the more information gathered before making decisions, the better the decisions will be. Women are better at soliciting information from their organizations.

3.2 Amy Edmondson: Turning Strangers into a Team

A powerful TED Talk was given by Amy Edmondson entitled *"How to turn a group of strangers into a team"* in 2017. She describes a list of behaviors for successful teams that supplements the previously discussed findings of Anita Woolley (2013).

Edmondson starts out by telling the story of a massive collapse of a copper mine in northern Chile in 2010. The collapse left 33 miners trapped half a mile underground with enough food for two men for 10 days. There was no drilling technology capable of drilling down through rock that hard to where they needed to be rescued from before they would be. It's not even known exactly where the men were. Still, all the men were in fact rescued alive. It took 70 days. And the success was largely because of the collective intelligence of an international team of diverse experts formed to tackle the problem.

Edmondson (2017) said that the team developed the absolutely critical qualities needed for highly productive teaming:

1. appropriate humility on the part of the leaders,
2. curiosity about anything and everything other people could bring, and
3. willingness to take risks and learn quickly.

Regarding humility: leaders at all levels were crystal clear that they didn't know the answers. They were willing to ask for help and this enabled expertise to be drawn, in this case, from around the world.

Edmondson further pointed out that there is often competition between individuals in a new situation and that it is vitally important to eliminate any sense of competition between them. There must be psychological safety so everyone speaks up and is given enthusiastic encouragement to do so. The most important takeaway, which we will see over and over again through this book, is that *humility* in leadership positions is vital. A humble leader is able to solicit information from subordinates in a non-confrontational manner. When it comes to making leadership decisions, the more information gathered, and the more people asked for advice, the wiser the decisions will be.

3.3 Lorna Davis: A Guide to Collaborative Leadership

Another deeply insightful TED Talk was given by Lorna Davis entitled "A guide to collaborative leadership," on February 14, 2020. She explains how great leadership comes from seeking advice from subordinates rather than presuming that you, as leader, have adequate answers. She described her progression from being a traditional top-down manager and CEO of several large corporations to becoming a collaborative leader. Davis gives the example of having lived in Shanghai, China for six years as CEO of the merged Danone and Kraft business selling Oreo cookies (among other things). She initially and unintentionally dominated meetings that were being held in English and was slightly intimidating (although she didn't know it at the time), and the company products were failing in China. Then she took a more retiring position in meetings, insisted that Chinese be spoken in the meetings, and required that every single person in the room speak up and volunteer an opinion. Thereafter they had a string of successes including the invention of the now-famous green tea Oreo cookie.

She says that when you, as a leader, stop trying to come up with the ideas yourself, and instead admit that you don't know the answers and want help from your team, meetings are much more productive, organizations become more creative, and overall productivity goes up. She went on to be CEO and Chairwoman of Danone Wave (Danone North America) with $6 billion revenue where she led the company to become a B Corp in 2018, which was the largest B Corp in the world at the time.[2]

3.4 Linda Hill: How to Manage for Collective Creativity

Similar advice was given by Harvard professor Linda Hill in a 2014 TEDxCambridge Talk entitled *"How to manage for collective creativity."* Professor Hill is co-author of Collective Genius, and she has studied some of the world's most creative companies. She and three other researchers

---

[2]B Corps commit to being serious about contributing to the communities where they operate as well as contributing to mitigation of global problems such as global warming.

studied 16 exceptional leaders (men and women) located in seven different countries in 12 different industries for a decade. Their conclusions, she said, can be summarized as follows:

> "If we want to build organizations that can innovate time and again, we must unlearn our conventional notions of leadership. Leading innovation is not about creating a vision, and inspiring others to execute it. . . [omitting much talking] . . . Our role as leaders is to set the stage, not perform on it. If we want to invent a better future, . . . Our task is to create the space where everybody's slices of genius can be unleashed and harnessed and turned into works of collective genius." (Hill, 2014)

This advice applies to all decision-making teams, not just creative teams: the more team members involved in making a decision, the better the decision is likely to be. . . Because they can draw on the collective intelligence of teams.

3.5 Alejandro Aravena: Bring the Community into the Process

Another story about collective intelligence comes from a TED Talk by Alejandro Aravena, TEDGlobal, 2014, entitled "My architectural philosophy? Bring the community into the process." Alejandro was challenged to build housing for 100 families in a city in northern Chile. Approximately 100 indigenous people had been living for years in a slum in the center of the city of Iquique that grew up around them. The government wanted to provide them decent housing with plumbing and infrastructure but didn't have a sufficient budget to do so. They gave Alejandro the challenge of building a housing development acceptable to the people with only half the money required to do the job to normal building standards.

Alejandro said there will be many more similar challenges over the next decade as people move to the city and it is forecast that nearly two billion city dwellers will be living below the poverty line by the year 2030. It follows that there could be considerable benefit if the problem was even partially solved. To solve it, he enlisted the help of the people living in the slums themselves. To begin with, the people refused to be moved into a high-rise which could have considerably reduced land costs. However, within a few days, the slum dwellers came up with an exceedingly ingenious solution. Basically, they recommended building half a house rather than a full house, but the architecture they chose left the space and partial framing for the other half of the house, which could be built later. The people thought they could probably afford to build the other half over time. This was a solution that would never have occurred to city planners or architects by themselves. It only came about because of the collective intelligence of the community. Alejandro's talk goes on to describe two other situations involving "community intelligence" in solving challenging environmental problems. Community intelligence is a form of collective intelligence.

3.6 Tom Wujec: Superior Designs with Movable Sticky Notes

Tom Wujec gave a TED Talk, June 2013, in Edinburgh Scotland, on "Got a wicked problem? First, tell me how you make toast." The talk was explicitly about designing systems and strategic planning using design techniques. But the talk also demonstrated the power of collective intelligence, but without using the terminology.

Specifically, Wujec has run hundreds of workshops in which he asks participants to draw a flow diagram on a single sheet of paper with nodes connecting stages of toast making. He then counts the number of nodes in the diagrams. The more detailed and meaningful diagrams have more nodes. The number of nodes typically range anywhere between 2 and 15. He then asks participants to use sticky notes or cards on which they can write to diagrams, with the flexibility of rearranging the notes. With the added flexibility of being able to rearrange the flow, participants produced more complex diagrams; typically with 50 percent more nodes. Having more complex systems diagrams is generally a reflection of better solutions, with greater utility and novelty. The histogram below summarizes this.

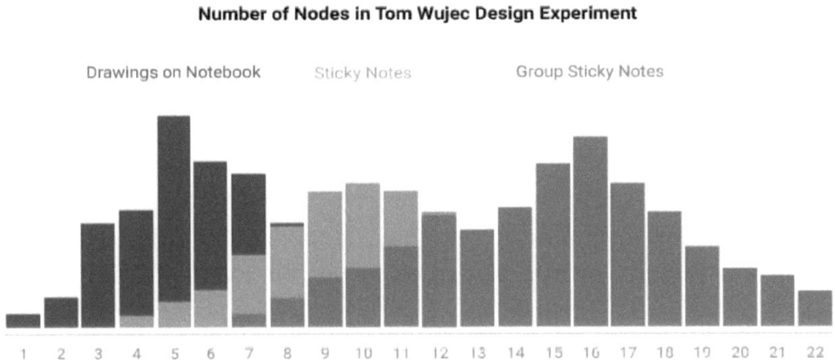

Figure 9: *Number of Nodes in Tom Wujec Design Experiment*

The histogram shows the number of nodes produced in drawings, the middle is using rearrangeable sticky notes; and the right is groups using sticky notes.

Source: ***Wujec, 2013***

Then he ran the same experiment except with groups designing and creating the flow diagrams. The result was even more complex systems diagrams, with another 50% increase in the number of nodes. Again, the more nodes, the better the design. He said, "When people work together under the right circumstances, group models are much better than individual models." (Wujec, 2013). In other words, teams produce better results than individuals working alone.

He went on to focus on strategic planning, brainstorming meetings, using movable sheets of paper with the publishing firm Rodale. Wujec said of Rodale: "They lost a bunch of money one year, and their executive team for three days visualized their entire practice. And what's interesting is that after visualizing the entire business, systems upon systems, they reclaimed 50 million dollars of revenue, and they also moved from a D rating to an A rating from their customers. Why?" (Wujec, 2013). Of course, the high-level answer is that collective intelligence is superior to the decision-making typical managerial groups. The secondary answer given by Wujec was that it was specifically because of the alignment between different departments and functions that resulted from discussing everything as a group. This is a rather striking discovery. Wujec clearly demonstrates the value of sharing and discussing information in larger groups, and also demonstrates a very useful tool: that having movable notes facilitates creativity. The movable notes principle can apply to all sorts of brainstorming activities, and clearly improves the collective intelligence of problem-solving teams.

3.7 Tom Wujec: The Spaghetti Challenge Prototyping vs. Planning

In his TED Talk 2010 "Build a tower, build a team," Tom Wujec describes running workshop experiments involving teams of four people who were given 18 minutes to build the tallest freestanding structure they can out of 20 sticks of uncooked spaghetti, one yard of tape, one yard of string, and a marshmallow which needs to be put on top of the freestanding structure.

The game has now been played thousands of times with different teams of four. The composition of the teams is purposefully varied to include MBAs, CEOs, mid-career professionals, mixed gender teams, and kindergarten children. The stunning result is that kindergarten children usually outperform adults!

We think that the reason for this is that adults spend too much time planning and not enough time experimenting. The children always execute a 'trial and error' process building several trial towers before the final one. The adults plan a long time and build one tower. The kids always beat adults (except for adult architects) that use a "plan first, then execute" strategy.

There are at least two lessons here for all companies with hopes of developing new products. The first is that listening to market feedback is a key method of growing organizational intelligence. This lesson is the heart of what is popularly known as the Lean Startup methodology. The idea is to create the minimal viable product, show it off in some shopping mall, and then get real-world feedback. The feedback gathered from this will influence how the product is iterated, then it will go through a second round of testing. The second lesson is that "planning is the kiss of death for innovation", as Peter Drucker said years ago. Of course, this is hyperbole, but the truth is that a little bit of planning followed by trial and error . . . followed by a little more planning, etc... is the ideal strategy. Larger and older organizations generally engage in too much planning and not enough doing.

You will recall that the 'iterative trial and error' approach was the reason that Steve Wozniak beat teams of engineers in early PC companies. It is also one of the reasons why two guys in a garage can often beat large companies in new product innovation.

Parenthetically, Wujec (2013) observes that when he puts a woman administrative assistant on a team of CEOs, the team does better. Wujec speculates that administrative assistants have some skill in managing their bosses. This, however, is not the right explanation. You will remember that Anita Woolley (2013) proved that teams generally do better with women on them with regards to tasks that do not require physical labor. Women are more empathetic than men on average, and this somehow helps teams to be more productive. Remember that diversity is one of the facilitating factors in collective intelligence.

3.8 Ray Dalio: Dot Collector Tool for Collective Intelligence

Ray Dalio in his 2017 TED Talk "How to build a company where the best ideas win" described a tool that's worth considering for brainstorming and exploiting collective intelligence in larger organizations. That tool is the 'Dot Collector.'

Dalio described it as a computer graphics-based tool showing a matrix of participants' names on both the horizontal and vertical axis. The cells in the matrix get numerical scores revealing how people on the vertical axis are scoring statements made by people on the horizontal axis during group discussions. The computer software sums up the degree of positivity accorded to any particular speaker on any particular topic. In addition, over time and many discussions, the participants' level of expertise is assessed, and their votes are given greater weight according to their level of expertise.

So there are situations when the rule "one person, one vote" is suboptimal, and Dalio shows how to improve upon it.

But in addition to adjusting weights on votes, Dalio also gives us a tool for real-time feedback to be used during discussions. Such a tool is likely to make discussions more efficient.

This is clearly not a publicly available tool, but for firms able to fund their own tools, the Dot Collector concept could be a model for their development.

3.9 Robert Kelly: How to Be a Star at Work

The technical foundations for the modern world of computers, artificial intelligence, and communication satellites can be traced to patents granted to Bell Labs more than 70 years ago for inventions of the transistor, lasers, solar cells, communication satellites, and other technologies. Clearly the scientists working at Bell Labs were brilliant.

What might it take to be a star performer among the world's best scientists at Bell Labs and perhaps be worthy of a Nobel Prize? Some research scientists at Bell Labs were thought to be 'an order of magnitude' (10 times) more productive than their peers. How is this even possible? Were these superstars possessed of extraordinary identifiable mental talents? Were they smarter than their peers (have higher IQs)? Did they have dominant personality types? Were they more self-confident? Were they driven and more ambitious than others? Have better leadership skills? Were they better organized? Work longer hours? Manage their time better? Were they better at organizational politics?

Robert Kelly studied these questions and reported his findings in the book *How to Be a Star at Work: 9 Breakthrough Strategies You Need to Succeed* first published in 1998.

Kelly actually investigated all the possibilities just listed and found little correlation with star performance. In other words, all the characteristics one would imagine are important to creativity and which employers often base hiring decisions, didn't seem to matter. Kelly eventually uncovered nine habits or practices that did seem to matter (listed below). But the most surprising habit was networking. He went on to say that of all the habits, networking must be considered absolutely essential for success in this day and age.

He further noted that, "networking, more than any other skill in the star performer model, can have a dramatic impact on the speed, quality, and quantity of your output. Without a high-quality network, you are unlikely to become a star performer. With one securely in place, you can leverage your knowledge base and give it a tremendous boost" (1998, 76).

Kelly gives an example in which two independent researchers were given a difficult problem to solve. One researcher went into his office, shut the door, and after a week of intense work, produced a brilliant solution full of mathematical derivations. The other researcher went into her office, and after a few phone calls had reached the world authority on the subject matter and had her solution within a day.

Networking and gathering other people's opinions is the heart of collective intelligence. Being good at networking means you have the means of exploiting collective intelligence. In my opinion, Kelly's star performers were actually exploiting collective intelligence. And their extraordinary performances showed just how powerful collective intelligence is relative to a single mind.

For the sake of completeness and respect for Robert Kelley's work, here are Kelly's nine talents that help people become "stars at work." (The wording is mine. I've paraphrased them.)

1. Initiative: don't wait to be told what to do by a boss. Figure out what's good for the organization and do it.
2. Networking: knowing who knows whom and actively cultivating a knowledge network.
3. Self-management: be well enough disciplined to spend your time on priority activities.
4. Perspective: understand what's good for your organization, not simply your small piece of it.
5. Followership: be helpful to others on their projects.
6. Leadership: let people know how they can help you.
7. Teamwork: don't be a loner, be a team player; help teams be productive.
8. Organizational Savvy: understand how power and information flow in your organization.
9. Show-and-tell: your value to your organization is in communicating what you know. Share your insights in memos, organized presentations as well as casual conversations (Kelley, 1998)

These should be included in any list of organizational genes that help lead to organizational intelligence. These are not, strictly speaking, organizational genes but personal behaviors. Nonetheless, these behaviors facilitate collective intelligence, and thereby contribute to organizational intelligence.

3.10 Key Points covered in Chapters 2 & 3

The checklist below is a summary of principles covered in chapters 2 & 3 that facilitate collective intelligence.

1. Team leaders ideally follow the ancient Greek wisdom of ethos, pathos, and logos.
   a. Ethos: leaders establish commonality of interest and that everyone has good reason to work together;
   b. Pathos: leaders articulate convincingly, with passion, that there is a serious problem to be solved

c. Logos: leaders must orchestrate the group's decision processes so that collective intelligence emerges.

2. Leader/Moderators must protect teams against "bad apples" (people with personal motives not aligned with the group), enforce turn-taking, terminate discussions, and formalize decisions.

3. Leader/Moderators must be humble and show genuine caring about opinions being offered.

4. Diversity in team membership can make teams smarter. Diversity comes from variety in the form of gender, race, religion, education, language, age, country of origin. . .. Almost everything that increases diversity also increases the team's aptitude for making good decisions and being creative.

5. Showing empathy between team members makes teams and organizations smarter.

6. Everyone must speak up in meetings and participate more or less equally. This applies to individuals and groups in an organization that may have information of relevance to a decision.

7. Discussion, not reporting, is mandatory because superior group creativity and idea synthesis happen only after discussion.

8. Optimism and goodwill must flow between team members.

9. Being helpful is more important than being right when it comes to discussing ideas.

10. Fact gathering from outside the team/group is essential. Google or other internet tools should be used to gather information and can be real-time or off-line.

11. Psychological safety must be an integral part of group discussions where psychological safety is defined to be freedom from potential social judgment or embarrassment.

12. Competition between team members is generally bad. Competition between teams is generally good.

13. Model building and prototyping should be part of product idea exploration when possible.

14. The use of supersized sticky notes (movable sheets of paper) to attach to walls can facilitate group creativity (see the comments in 2.11 by Tom Wujec).

15. Having a noble or socially responsible vision helps, e.g., Google's vision statement.
16. Being part of a team helps with motivation, creativity and productivity
17. Giving employees more control helps, e.g., employee participation in setting objectives allocating the budget.
18. Compliments and positive feedback help on daily interactions, and employee performance reviews every six months work better than annual reviews.
19. Civility in the workplace, outside of meetings, helps.
20. In framing high-level objectives, senior management must avoid being too precise. There must always be room for implementers to be creative and show their intelligence.

This last item is the Japanese management style, which is generally quite effective. The Japanese are famous for 'managing by metaphor'. The senior executives will say something like "Remember the slogan: The Theory of Automobile Evolution," and not say anything more precise (Takeuchi, Nonaka, 1991). This actually happened at Honda during the development of one of their more popular cars. The idea is that the creativity and intelligence of managers at all levels should be given the chance to fill in the details. This circumvents the limitations of top-down management by allowing more minds to be involved in strategic planning and innovation. This is one way of exploiting organizational intelligence, which is the subject of the next section.

To summarize: Chapters 2 and 3 are all about techniques for accessing collective intelligence in groups and teams. The examples show, over and over again, that better decisions can be made by groups than by individuals. The chapters give guidelines, behaviors and conditions that increase the collective intelligence of groups and builds the basis for organizational intelligence.

Chapter 4 introduces organizational intelligence, which benefits from collective intelligence, but deals with organizational performance rather than team performance.

SECTION 2: ORGANIZATIONAL INTELLIGENCE

Businesses and nations are constantly evolving, as they must, being driven by the same laws of nature that created life. Those organizations with the highest intelligence survive longer and have more prosperous citizens or employees. Therefore, as citizens and employees, it's in our best interest to help our organizers understand the genes that give rise to improved organizational intelligence.

CHAPTER 4: THE RISE AND FALL OF GREAT COMPANIES

Shakespeare wrote in *Julius Caesar*, "There is a tide in the affairs of men, which taken at the flood, leads on to fortune. Omitted, all the voyage of their life is bound in shallows and in miseries. On such a full sea are we now afloat. And we must take the current when it serves or lose our ventures." (Act-IV, Scene-III).

Civilization is in fact evolving and evolving at an exponentially increasing rate. The force behind this evolution is automation. However, there is a paradox in this apparent progress. For employees, chances of becoming unemployed are increasing because of automation. For entrepreneurs and businessmen, on the other hand, this is the moment of the tide in their affairs. There are more opportunities than ever.

The progress of civilization, in fact, means machines will be generating more wealth with less manpower than ever before using automation. The most potent technologies for automation, the source of the tide, were developed (and are still being developed) in Silicon Valley. Silicon Valley is phenomenal, to put it mildly.

The top 15 companies in Silicon Valley had sales of $1.35 trillion in 2020, which, if they were a nation, would rank them between Spain and Mexico in terms of a global GDP ranking. Silicon Valley has generated more patents per unit area than any other place on earth. Half the world's billionaires lived in Silicon Valley circa 2020 (this may no longer be true). Nations around the world have tried to understand what gives Silicon Valley its dynamism and power. Factors are listed at the end of this chapter, but first a little history provides context.

Silicon Valley gets its name, and much of its success, because of Intel. Intel was founded in 1968 in the shadow of Stanford University. It was the first company to successfully commercialize large-scale integrated circuits using silicon, hence the name Silicon Valley. Intel used its LSI technology to develop the world's first microprocessors (in competition with Texas Instruments) which created the PC revolution. PCs became ubiquitous and formed the platform for the internet, smart mobile phones, big data, AI, automation and robotics, all of which now are transforming the lives of more people more rapidly than any other peacetime development in history.

The next few pages provide a brief history lesson on the little-known role played by Xerox Corporation in the chain of events that led to the phenomenal commercial success of the microprocessor. It should be interesting because of its historical role, but more importantly it introduces the business dynamic of the rise and fall of great businesses.

The once mighty Xerox Corporation, headquartered in Rochester, New York, decided to set up its West Coast R&D lab in Palo Alto, California, on Stanford University land in 1970, before the invention of the first microprocessor chips. They called it Palo Alto Research Center, PARC. Before the first microprocessor chips were invented, PARC had conceived and built the first modern PCs and supportive technologies that laid the groundwork for the PC revolution. They invented laser printing, ethernet, the first notebook computers, the graphical user interface (bitmapped graphics allowing desktop metaphor icons) of the Apple Macintosh line; object-oriented programming (the basis of all modern programming languages); what would become the Windows operating system; Bravo which became Microsoft Word, and other pillars of the modern computing world. They did all this before Apple and Microsoft were founded. This is the time at which pundits sometimes say Xerox "fumbled the future," as described in the book "Fumbling the future: How Xerox invented, then ignored, the first personal computer," (Alexander, Smith, 1988).

Xerox inherited this criticism because they didn't commercially exploit their inventions, but rather allowed them to leak out into the community to startups, prominently Apple and Microsoft.

Note that Apple and Microsoft, as of this writing, are two of the most valuable companies in the world and they grew from rank startups in 1976 indirectly using PARC inventions. I hope the irony of this is not lost on you[3].

Xerox would have liked to have benefited from the ascendancy of personal computers. But there was something in their corporate genes that prevented them from exploiting this opportunity. It is also the case that they tried to enter the computer business by acquiring Scientific Data Systems. But SDC, along with all the other incumbent computer companies, did not adapt quickly enough to accommodate personal computers, because they were focused on larger commercial applications of computing, not small gaming and personal applications.

As mentioned in the preface, this is typical corporate behavior. Large successful companies, like Xerox, usually don't recognize disruptive technologies until it is too late to exploit them or to avoid being disrupted by them. The brilliant Harvard business theorist, Clayton Christensen, studied this universal phenomenon because it is so prevalent and sought to explain it in his famous book, *The Innovator's Dilemma*. We will discuss it in Chapter 4.2 below. He said, in essence, that it all boils down to the law of resource dependency which says that existing customers of the company indirectly determine what projects get funded. Projects/products far afield from existing customers don't get funded.

Nonetheless, Xerox did try to commercialize the PARC work. They spent more than $850 million on the STAR workstation which was essentially the Xerox precursor of the Apple Macintosh (which retailed for $2500). The problem was the retail cost of the STAR was intended to be about $16,000.

And this brings up a universal aspect of competing with startups. Established companies simply cannot compete in new product development with startups with their low overheads and minimal bureaucracy. Consider Steve Wozniak, the designer of the Apple II, the popularity of which enabled Apple to go public. Wozniak designed the Apple II by himself making trial designs he would show off to hobbyists at the Homebrew Computer Club

[3]At the time that Microsoft was formed it was not using PARC inventions, but this came later with the adoption of Windows, Microsoft Word, and object-oriented programming. Similarly, Apple took the basis for the Macintosh computer line which debuted in 1984 from Xerox inventions circa 1974.

at Stanford University where he got feedback. He perfected hardware and software designs using trial and error rather than planning.

Competing with Wozniak in 1977 were at least a half-dozen large companies attempting to build the first PCs at the same time. But established company engineers needed first to make a plan, rough out a design and task timeline, wait for approvals, and then proceed to deliver what they promised. Such 'planning' always inhibits the speed of product development and innovation, not only because of bureaucratic delays, but because it forces employees to deliver what they promise and doesn't give them the latitude to go off and pursue something they just discovered midway through a plan.

In any case, the Apple II completely blew away all the competition and became the gold standard model for future PCs, including IBM's first entry into the PC market in 1981.The Apple II kicked off the first of three new technology waves in Silicon Valley (1976—Apple, Microsoft enabled by microprocessor technology; 1995—Amazon, eBay, PayPal, Google, Yahoo!—enabled by the graphics browser internet; 2009—Airbnb, Uber, WhatsApp—enabled by smart mobile phones). These waves were clearly based on new technology developments.

The profound question is why were established technology companies not involved? Not a single one of these above-mentioned corporate giants was started by an existing technology company. All of them were started in garages or apartments. To emphasize this question, note that Wozniak offered to give HP the plans for, *and ownership rights to*, the Apple I in 1976. (Wozniak was working at HP at the same time he was designing the Apple I as a hobby.) HP turned him down. It is so ironic that the world's most valuable company, as of 2020, started out as a big company reject.

What lessons can we draw from these examples?

The first lesson might be that to maximize innovation, companies should hire and support bright people and get out of the way, as Xerox PARC did. But this would need to be married to a second lesson, the one that Xerox missed.

The second lesson might be that innovation in established companies (e.g., Xerox) should be provided with an entrepreneurial path to commercialization. This would probably be accomplished by creating a new independent company, a startup. The parent company would take equity in the startup and give it access to the novel technology. Currently prototypes developed in company R&D labs usually stay in the R&D labs because the costs of commercialization are prohibitive. Rank startups always have dramatically lower commercialization costs. And, just as important, prototypes in R&D labs always require a great deal more applied R&D before they are actually ready for the marketplace. This applied R&D is what entrepreneurs do better than large companies because they must face real world market feedback more quickly.

A third lesson is actually a question: what is it about well-managed corporations that makes them blind to new opportunities and subject to disruption? What needs to happen inside a company for it to avoid disruption as new technologies are emerging? The answers are subtle and involve the way organizational intelligence ebbs and flows inside companies. The only way to understand it is through examples of the rise and fall of companies.

4.1 Why Do Great, Well-Managed Companies Fail?

Why do great, well-managed companies decline?

Consider Sears Roebuck. If ever there was a well-managed company, it was Sears Roebuck in the 1960s. Nonetheless, Sears declined and was eventually driven out of business by competition, principally by Walmart, itself a startup in 1963.

Sears Roebuck was regarded for decades as one of the most astutely managed retailers in the world. At its zenith, Sears accounted for more than two percent of all retail sales in the United States. It pioneered several innovations critical to the success of today's most admired retailers: for example, supply chain management, store brands, catalog retailing, and credit card sales.

This rise and fall is typical for the majority of companies, even for the best-run companies which practice the best-known management principles taught in the best business schools. And declines occur in all genres: product development companies, retail companies, and service providing companies. The same management that brought companies to large-scale success is still there during the decline. So, something is going on that is not adequately understood, but experts certainly have opinions.

Let's see what the experts say.

4.2 What the Experts Say

4.2.1 Richard Foster and Sarah Kaplan: Creative Destruction

The rise and fall of companies were explored in a book entitled *Creative Destruction* written by Richard Foster and Sarah Kaplan of McKinsey and Company, published in 2001. At that time, they could find no corporations that had consistently beat the market year after year beyond an upper limit of approximately 15 years. They also found that 75% of companies failed before their tenth birthday.

What Foster and Kaplan found was that a 'built to last' company is a myth (despite the book by that title, see next chapter). There are no companies with share prices that consistently outperform the average stock for more than a few years. Many of the better companies may outperform the market for a few years, five years perhaps; and the really excellent companies a little longer, perhaps as much as 15 years, but almost never keep up with the market average (S&P 500, the Dow Jones, or Russell 2000) - few exceptions to this rule, Microsoft and Apple, are special cases that will be addressed later.

To explain the principle from a different angle, they found Standard & Poor's roster of America's largest companies kept changing because initially rapidly growing companies kept eventually dropping off. For example, most of the companies on the S&P 500 in the year 1957 had dropped off by 1997. More precisely, they found that 426 companies dropped off and only 74 remained, over a 40-year period of time. There are outlier companies like GE, IBM, DuPont, P&G, Coca-Cola, and Kellogg's that have done well for more than 100 years. But they are not doing as well as the market averages. And for a larger number of previously big-name companies, they have indeed gone out of business entirely. The general rule is that most successful companies will go into gradual decline a few years after their zenith.

Joseph Schumpeter popularized the term "creative destruction" (1942), to describe a homeostatic balance of companies that were continually dying while others were springing up. It is the inspiration for the title of the book by Kaplan and Foster. However, the theory doesn't explain why this might be happening, only that it does happen. With physical product producing companies, you might ascribe business rise and fall to a popular product and its lifecycle. In the beginning, when the product is new and no one has it, growth will be rapid; but later the company might slow down when the market saturates for the product. This reasoning doesn't apply to retail companies like Sears and Roebuck, A&P, JCPenney, Kroger, Kmart, Kodak, RadioShack, etc. But all of these companies are in decline or out of business.

4.2.2 Jerry Porras and Jim Collins: Built to Last

The possibility that having the right foundation in a company could allow it to avoid decline was explored in one of the most popular and influential business books of the last 30 years, *Built to Last: Successful Habits of Visionary Companies,* written by Stanford professors Jerry Porras and Jim Collins and first published in 1994.

In their work, Porras and Collins investigated 200 long-lived companies. These long-lived companies were analyzed and pruned away until 18 were left, the best of the best. The authors set out to determine what allowed these companies to be long-term survivors. They were looking for "timeless, fundamental principles and patterns that might apply across eras" (1994). Most businesspeople of the time would have agreed with the excellence of the companies on this list, which included IBM, Citicorp, Johnson & Johnson, Boeing, General Electric, Disney, Walmart, Hewlett-Packard, and ten others. In order to grasp what makes these companies special and different, the authors identified same-industry comparison companies that did not do so well but were nonetheless successful and respectable. These comparison companies included the likes of Chase Manhattan Bank, which was compared to Citicorp; McDonnell Douglas, which was compared to Boeing; and Texas Instruments, which was compared to Hewlett-Packard.

Collins and Porras and their Stanford graduate students then undertook a massive data-gathering and analysis project. As a group, they covered more than 100 books, including autobiographies, histories, and exposés, and in excess of 3,000 other documents including articles from company publications and mass media, including, amongst others: *Business Week, Fortune, Forbes, The Wall Street Journal,* and *The New York Times.* They conducted personal interviews and looked at case studies from Harvard and Stanford.

When it was all done, they identified six factors that they called "timeless principles." They are:

1. having a strong core ideology that guides the company's decisions and behavior

2. building a strong corporate culture
3. setting audacious goals that inspire and stretch people
4. developing people and promoting them from within
5. creating a spirit of experimentation and risk-taking
6. driving for excellence (1994)

This is certainly an intuitively appealing list of objectives for a company's management team. It contains the things that we know we should do as employees and managers. In any case, history has shown that the most important things for long-term companies' survival are not on this list. This is made clear in the research of Phil Rosenzweig.

4.2.2.1 Phil Rosenzweig: The Halo Effect

In his excellent book *The Halo Effect*, Phil Rosenzweig looked into the Porras/Collins study and found the following: for the five years following the completion of the data-gathering portion of the "built to last" study, namely 1991–1995, only 8 of the 18 outperformed the S&P market average. The other ten companies didn't keep up with the S&P 500 market average. In other words, if you were an investor, you would have been better off to short sell the very companies Collins and Porras identified as the best companies in America based on following their principles! (1994).

But that's not all. Rosenzweig then compared the ten-year period 1991-2000 and found that only six companies out of 16 kept up with the S&P 500, and the remaining ten didn't keep up. Rosenzweig also looked at profitability, defined as the operating profit as a percentage of assets. For the first five years, only five companies improved their profitability and 11 had declining profitability; presumably, the others didn't have publicly available records.

The failure of the companies that presumably practiced the six timeless principles is worth paying attention to given the huge publicity that the book received, and the amount of work that went into extracting those principles. In fact, most of the business community would have agreed with Porras and Collins (1994) in their choice of companies to epitomize corporate longevity. Nonetheless, the evidence is consistent and strong. These great companies couldn't avoid the seemingly universal rule of 'old age decline' with regard to their company fortunes. These results only deepen the mystery of why mature corporations' decline.

4.2.3 Tom Peters and Bob Waterman: In Search of Excellence

Another set of authors set out to find the rules of governance that lead to greatness in the book *In Search of Excellence* The book was a huge success. It would be difficult to overstate the popularity of the book in the business world for at least 20 years after its publication in 1982. Its authors, Tom Peters and Bob Waterman, were consultants working for McKinsey and Co. when they started the book in 1977.

They launched their study to answer a fundamental question: Why are some companies more successful than others? The strategy was to identify truly excellent companies (they identified 62 initially) and then study them to understand why they were 'excellent.' After some initial research, they reduced the number of companies to be analyzed in depth to 43. These excellent companies were all the darlings of Wall Street and the business community at large. Their public images as well as their share price appreciation would rank them among the 'best of the best.' To identify them, the authors used the extensive databases of McKinsey and Co.; and they talked to academics, other McKinsey consultants, and business leaders. They claimed their process for selecting the companies was in keeping with the McKenzie practices of being quantitative, rigorous, systematic, and objective.

Most people were convinced and the back jacket of the most recent printing of the book, by Harper Business Essentials (HarperCollins Publishers) captures the sentiment. It reads: "The Greatest Business Book of all Time (Bloomsbury UK), *In Search of Excellence* has long been a must-have for the boardroom, business school, and bedside table."

Based on their detailed analysis of America's best-run companies from a diverse array of business sectors, *In Search of Excellence* describes the basic principles of management: action-stimulating, people-oriented, profit-maximizing practices that made these organizations successful.

The book announced the "Eight Practices of America's Best Companies" (1982, 86)

1. A bias for action – a preference for doing something—anything—rather than sending a question through cycles and cycles of analysis and committee reports.

2. Staying close to the customer – learning your customers' preferences and catering to them.

3. Autonomy and entrepreneurship – breaking the corporation into two or more smaller companies and encouraging them to think independently and competitively.

4. Productivity through people – creating in all employees the awareness that their best efforts are essential and that they will share in the rewards of the company's success.

5. Stick to the knitting – maintaining focus on the business the company knows best.

6. Simple form, lean staff – reducing the number of administrative layers and making do with fewer people at the upper levels.

7. Simultaneous loose–tight properties – fostering a climate where there is dedication to the central values of the company combined with a tolerance for all employees who accept those values.

At the time they published the book, the authors were convinced that if managers followed the rules above, they would create excellent companies that would survive a long time. And they had evidence that the 42 companies they identified did, indeed, follow these rules. The book instantly went to the top of the best-seller lists and stayed there for many months. Peters and Waterman were judged to be business gurus if not geniuses.

The list of excellent companies included names like Boeing, Delta Air Lines, Digital Equipment, Hewlett-Packard, IBM, Procter & Gamble, 3M, and Caterpillar.

So how did the excellent companies actually perform after being identified? Again, we need to look at the work of Phil Rosenzweig.

4.2.3.1 Phil Rosenzweig: The Halo Effect

Here we turn, again, to the research presented by Phil Rosenzweig in *The Halo Effect*. He looked at 35 of the 43 companies identified as excellent by Peters and Waterman (these being the only companies for which he could get public financial details). He computed the shareholder return, which is the percent change in stock price plus dividends covering a five-year period beginning in 1980 - the last year covered by the data in *In Search of Excellence*. Rosenzweig found that only 12 companies grew faster than the S&P 500. For 23 of the 35 companies, he was able to analyze that they underperformed the market! Let this sink in for a moment. Two-thirds of the companies identified as being excellent underperformed the market.

Rosenzweig continued. He expanded the time frame to cover the ten-year period from 1980 to 1989, and he got much the same result: 18 of the companies failed to keep up with the market, and only 13 outperformed the market[4]. This is an incredible result because it showed that these intuitively pleasing genes for governing a company did nothing to prevent decline. Once again, investors would have been better off selling short the stock in the list of America's most excellent companies from the moment they were identified in In Search of Excellence rather than purchasing shares in these companies.

The irony is abundantly clear, but the reasons behind it are anything but. What happened to these stellar companies to cause such a surprising decline in their performance? When you see this result for the first time, you would probably say that there is something wrong with the stock prices. These excellent companies surely wouldn't have had such drastic declines in the actual operation of their companies. Would they?

To answer this objection, Rosenzweig looked at another measure, namely, captured profitability, which is a company's operating income as a percent of its total assets. For the same five-year time period covered in his original analysis (1980-1984), 30 of the 35 excellent companies showed a decline in captured profitability. Only five of the 'excellent' companies actually became more profitable after they were identified as the best in the nation. This declining profitability is even more dramatic than the declining share value because it drives home the fact that this wasn't just an aberration in share price valuations. The operating performance of the ensemble of excellent companies really did decline.

So, what does this say about the Eight Practices of America's Best Companies? Did these companies actually follow these practices in the first place? Were the Eight Practices really important? Did their implementation change all of a sudden? Did the management teams, seeing themselves honored in the book *In Search of Excellence*, become filled with hubris and stop trying hard enough? These are rhetorical questions, and we cannot know the answers to them. But we can be confident that management did not suddenly become incompetent. We can also be pretty sure that technological advances didn't come along in the hands of competitors to drive them into decline. It can also be assumed that the companies didn't stop practicing the Eight Practices. It's just that the Eight Practices are not as important as something else . . . yet to be identified.

[4]Public data was unavailable for the other companies.

So, are the Eight Practices relatively useless? Quite the contrary, the Eight Practices may be important, it's simply that something else is more important than all these eight combined. So, we must ask the question again: Why do great companies decline and die?

4.2.4 Clayton Christensen: The Innovator's Dilemma

Christensen explicitly tackled the question of technology disruption and corporate demise in his book, *The Innovator's Dilemma*, first published in 1997 by the Harvard Business School Press. Christensen at the time was an associate professor of business administration at the Harvard Business School. Christensen was one of the most insightful business theorists of the 21st century. Unfortunately, he died early in 2020. His primary contribution to humanity was an explanation of why companies are driven out of business by new companies using disruptive technology. He called his explanation a 'disruption-based model'

To give you some appreciation of his brilliance, an article published in *TechCrunch*, by Thomas Thurston, in 2014, by the title of "Christensen Vs. Lepore: A Matter of Fact", ''Disruption-based models [Christensen's theories] had produced more than 3,400 blind, real-world predictions about business survival or failure." The article then goes on to say, "Put into perspective, the models have now made more predictions than all US venture capital deals over the past five years combined, with a predictive accuracy more than 2.5X greater than the venture capital industry as a whole" (Thurston, 2014). There is no other business theorist that can claim anything close to this; although, this book augments Christensen's theories which could significantly increase the predictive power of the models.

In his book, Christensen noted: "the harsh reality of the business world is that the decline of showcase companies is, in fact, the rule rather than the exception: Most big companies end up declining after having their decade or two as market leaders. And the decline of great companies is almost always attributed by the media to be the result of a failure in management. But this explanation cannot be right. It's usually the same management that led the company to its zenith in the first place" (1997, page).

Christensen also observed that the disruption and decline of companies always involves the use of new technology in the hands of startups that take business away from incumbents. He asked: Why is it that so few companies reinvent themselves to become leaders in new market segments?

Why do corporations fail to make the leap and adapt to changing market conditions? Quoting Christensen himself from the introduction to the book, Christensen noted that: "This book is about the failure of companies to stay atop their industries when they confront certain types of market and technological change. It's not about the failure of simply any company, but of good companies—the kinds that many managers have admired and tried to emulate, the companies known for their abilities to innovate and execute... It is about well-managed companies that have their competitive antenna up, listen astutely to their customers, invest aggressively in new technologies, and still lose market dominance" (1997).

Such seemingly unaccountable failures happen in industries that move fast and in those that move slow; in those built on electronics technology and those built on chemical and mechanical technology; in manufacturing and in-service industries. Christensen covered the evolution of the computing industry in gory detail. He described how IBM, the world's most powerful technology company in the 1970s, made its fortune in mainframe computers. Then DEC came along with Data General, Prime, Wang, Hewlett-Packard, and Nixdorf to manufacture and sell minicomputers that ate into the mainframe market. IBM certainly had the resources to dominate the minicomputer market, but it did not. Then Apple Computer came along with a plethora of PC startups and stole the market from the minicomputer benefactors; they all collapsed in approximately 1988. None of the minicomputer companies survived the PC revolution. This time IBM decided to play in the PC market for about a decade before abandoning it. IBM practically went out of business in the early 1990s having had its mainframe market decimated by PCs.

Christensen observes that, with each generation of computing technology, the companies that dominated the industry failed to make the transition to the next generation. In each case, newcomers and startups became the dominant players in the new industries. And these "startups" became huge. And just as important, the older incumbents declined. Christensen goes on to describe other sensational companies that had remarkable growth followed by remarkable decline, none more fascinating than the disk drive industry. Between 1977 and 1994, the disk drive industry came up with no fewer than 116 distinct innovations, of which 111 were what Christensen terms 'sustaining'. These sustaining innovations made distinct improvements in storage capacity, speed of access, insulation from jarring, and reductions in size. The sustaining innovations helped the incumbents to improve their existing product lines. However, the remaining five innovations were disruptive, and each of these five innovations caused the collapse of an incumbent and gave the innovative company, essentially, the entire market.

And in each case, the incumbent had in its research laboratories, samples of the very technology that would later cause their demise.

Christensen specifically noted that: "well-managed firms such as those cited above, good management was the most powerful reason they failed to stay atop their industries. Precisely because these firms listened to their customers, invested aggressively in new technologies that would provide their customers more and better products of the sort they wanted, and because they carefully studied market trends and systematically allocated investment capital to innovations that promised the best returns, they lost their positions of leadership" (1997, 94).

He finally comes to this conclusion: to explain why incumbents do not defend themselves by adopting the new technology themselves… the theory of resource dependency. He wrote, "while managers may think they control the flow of resources within their firms, in the end it is really customers and investors who dictate how money will be spent because companies with investment patterns that don't satisfy their customers and investors don't survive. The highest performing companies, in fact, are those that are the best at this, that is, they have well developed systems for killing ideas that their customers don't want. As a result, these companies find it very difficult to invest adequate resources in disruptive technologies—lower margin opportunities that their customers don't want—until their customers want them. And by then it is too late" (1997, 232).

The resource dependency theory states that the customers of the firm indirectly control the funding for programs inside the company. If you are an innovator inside a company and you want funds to develop new technology, or to execute a new business model based on new technology, you will find that the funds are simply not available . . . unless they can be shown to serve the existing customer base. Thus, radical change becomes impossible, and radical change is what is required to avoid the kind of disruption these companies all faced. As Christensen humorously puts it in his lectures at Harvard concerning the management challenges inside the incumbent companies, "What would you do? Listen to your customers, or take a gamble on a product that your customers don't want that would wreck your profit margins?" (Christensen, 2001).

Most importantly: Clayton Christensen concludes that corporations decline because of the law of resource dependency. This law states that companies are competitively locked into serving their existing customer bases, and that this leaves them with insufficient financial resources to innovate in technologies that lie far from their current markets.

4.2.5 Summary

Let's summarize what our popular thought leaders have said.

In the first book, *Creative Destruction* (2001), we started out with claims made by Sarah Kaplan and Richard Foster that mature companies almost never outperform the market for more than 15 years. This suggests that corporate declines are the norm.

There are three explanations:

A) This may be a consequence of how the market is defined. The market (i.e., the S&P 500) contains younger, smaller companies. Younger and smaller companies appreciate more rapidly than mature companies, on average. Thus, the market actually grows faster than the share price of a mature company. Thus, not keeping up with the market doesn't mean the major companies are actually declining, rather they are just not growing as fast as younger companies.

B) The other reason for decline may derive from actual decline in an absolute sense. The causes for absolute decline may be that younger competitors are taking business away, or it may mean that the market size is diminishing due to the evolution of consumer demand.

C) As companies mature, they institute procedures that optimize performance at the expense of adaptability. Thus, as technology and markets evolve, mature companies do not adapt fast enough to remain competitive.

In the second book, *Built to Last: Successful Habits of Visionary Companies* (Collins, 1994), we saw that most of the 18 mature companies (including the corporate giants IBM, Citicorp, Johnson & Johnson, Boeing, General Electric, and Disney) underperformed the market, and had decreasing profitability as well. These great companies are still around but are not doing as well as younger companies. The authors identified corporate "genes" that most people would think would help companies be long-term survivors and outperform the market. But the research done by Phil Rosenzweig (2007) showed that these genes which they called "enduring principles" were simply insufficient to guide companies to achieve superior performance.

In the third book *In Search of Excellence*, (Peters, Waterman, 1982), the authors identified habits and practices that should constitute good genes that would help companies succeed. However, we saw that only 12 companies of 35 firms grew faster than the S&P 500 after the book was published. Twenty-three of the 35 companies underperformed the market!

And there is more bad news. 30 of the 35 excellent companies showed a decline in profitability in the decade immediately following the publication of the book! Again, the enduring principles selected by the expert authors were insufficient to guide companies to achieve superior performance. It's safe to say that the corporate genes *did not* accomplish what the authors were seeking, namely, a list of organizational practices that, if followed, would lead to superior performance.

In the fourth book *The Innovator's Dilemma,* (Christensen, 1997), Christensen noted that incumbents get disrupted by startups because of "the law of resource dependency" and "the law of attraction of higher profitability".

1. The law of resource dependency states that existing customers of firms cause the firms to focus on new product development on satisfying their needs. Since disruptive products are generally invisible to the customer base, they don't get developed.
2. This second law states that there is a general tendency for incumbent companies to 'flee up-market' when confronted with competition at the low-end of their market. That is to say, companies favor developing higher quality, higher-margin products and ceding lower quality, lower-margin products to competitors. However, the lower quality products produced by the startups gradually become higher quality. This eventually takes away market share from the incumbents. Eventually, the incumbents find themselves "disrupted" and out of business.

Christensen's arguments say, in essence, that the failures of big companies that kill them are failures of resource allocation and inability to adjust internal cost structures to accommodate entirely new technologies.

Christensen gives the example of computer disk drive manufacturers that he studied. All had samples of disruptive technologies in their labs. They had more resources than the startups. They just couldn't get their costs down enough to compete with the startups.

As a result, all hardware manufacturers were disrupted, and many driven out of business even though they had the disruptive technology in-house. Christensen thinks that incumbent internal cost structures were the Achilles' heels that killed them. Incumbent infrastructures and cost structures simply can't compete with newly constructed efficient cost structures in the hands of a startup.

In conclusion, we have just looked at the advice offered by the most celebrated business thinkers of our time to companies trying to avoid disruption or gradual decline. Some offered organizational genes which should have helped, but they don't appear to have had much impact on business. Christensen (1997), on the other hand, offered helpful strategic planning insights, but companies have generally not changed their practices to accommodate his insights.

This book will be offering alternative answers to the questions about corporate decline when we look at the impact organizational intelligence.

As a first step to a deeper understanding of how to avoid decline and/or disruption, we consider the paradox of strong leadership, the kind of leadership sought to sustain growth and prevent decline.

4.3 The Paradox of Charismatic Leadership

Traditionally, the heads of major corporations are selected on the basis of personal charisma and their track records. We all instinctively admire good-looking, healthy, 'charismatic' men and women, and we instinctively are more likely to follow charismatic leaders. Consequently, charismatic people are the overwhelming favorites to head companies.

Malcolm Gladwell once said he (or perhaps his assistant) called up the executive offices of the 500 biggest companies on the New York Stock Exchange and asked for the height of their CEO. It turned out that more than 90% of the CEOs were more than 6′2″ tall, roughly the height of basketball players on a typical professional basketball team. But does personal charisma really help performance as a corporate leader?

Somebody actually studied companies with exceptionally charismatic leaders. Before we describe the study, visualize the following situation:

Suppose you are on the Board of Directors of a firm that has been profitable for at least the last five years. The company has been growing and outperforming the competition. The CEO of the company has been described in glowing terms by the press and is quite ambitious. The CEO thinks he could do an even better job if he had the titles of President and Chairman of the Board. So, you and the other board members agree to these promotions. What are the risks in making such a promotion? Would witness impact the board's fiduciary responsibility to the pension funds that have invested their money in their company?

This is exactly the situation that arose in the EU and the USA between 1997 and 2003 with nearly half of the 100 best-performing companies in both geographic entities being headed by exceptionally charismatic leaders. The CEOs were rewarded for their outstanding success by being given the titles Chairman of the Board, President, and CEO. The problem is that the spectacular performance did not continue. The details came from a rigorous study of corporate failures carried out by Gilbert Probst and Sebastian Raisch: *"Organizational Crisis: The Logic of Failure."* (2005) They found that the biggest business collapses in Europe and the USA around the year 2000 were correlated with managerial power being concentrated in the hands of highly charismatic CEOs. It looked as if there was a negative causal relationship between charisma and performance.

The details are as follows: the authors studied the 100 largest organizational crises over five years, starting in 1998 in Europe and the United States. They started with the 100 largest organizational collapses measured in decline in share values of these publicly traded companies and then they shortlisted the top 50 losers of shareholder value. The firms they chose had lost a combined US$2.5 trillion over the five-year period of time 1998–2003, an amount exceeding the national GDP of most nations on the planet. So, these were big companies. They included WorldCom, Enron, Conseco, Global Crossing, United Airlines, and Kmart, which all collapsed, and between them had 125,000 layoffs and lost $300 billion in corporate value. Other giants included ABB, AT&T, Daimler Chrysler, France Telecom, Time Warner, and Vivendi Universal, which also collapsed and between them lost $510 billion. This happened after years of steady growth. In fact, this steady growth only added to the stature of the CEOs.

The authors began by considering the possibility that the large failures were due to structural dynamics or externalities and that consequently it was not the leadership that was at fault. They immediately demonstrated that this could not be the cause because the companies fell off a financial cliff at the height of their success, which is certainly not part of a natural cycle. Their primary conclusion was that the companies headed by highly successful, charismatic CEOs lost half their value simply because of leadership. Specifically, ABB, Enron, Swissair, and WorldCom dominated their respective markets and had done so for a decade or more. It was unthinkable at the time that they could end up in bankruptcy within a few months. All these companies had been enjoying substantial growth prior to their collapse and the CEOs took credit for the growth. They typically took on triple titles: Chairman of the Board, CEO, and President. The press, analysts, and shareholders were applauding these larger-than-life corporate heroes. Apparently, the CEOs increasingly believed in their own infallibility and behaved as autocrats making unilateral decisions. And that was their undoing. They basically destroyed the corporate intelligence that could have been there if they and others hadn't believed in their sole judgment. In other words, the largest corporate failures in Europe and the USA over a five-year period (1998–2003), seemed to be caused by having leadership by charismatic, overconfident, autocratic leaders.

Further evidence that strong charismatic leadership is inferior to humble leadership is shown in a study carried out by Jim Collins (2001) He found that declining companies can be turned into highly successful companies by humble leadership. In Chapter 5.1, we discuss the book *Good to Great* by Jim Collins, but a quote from this book applies perfectly here as well. The author states: "we found the only leaders who turned companies around [from decline to unmitigated success] in the history of the S&P 500 [between 1967 and 1997] and it wasn't their towering personalities, it was their humility" (2001, 73).

The resolution of the above seeming paradoxes is that humble leadership tends to bring out the collective intelligence of the organization, whereas strong charismatic leadership tends to kill it. This doesn't mean that charismatic leaders are incapable of setting the stage for others to generate ideas. It's just that they usually don't do it. Further evidence comes from Sydney Finkelstein's *Why Smart Executives Fail* (2003), and his article published in Forbes magazine in January 2012 entitled "Seven Habits of Spectacularly Unsuccessful Executives." The author had researched over 50 successful large companies that crashed dramatically, including Enron, Tyco, WorldCom, Rubbermaid, Research in Motion, and Schwinn. Finkelstein came up with the seven behaviors that he says were common to all the failed CEOs. The following seven habits are taken from the article:

Bad Habit #1: The failed CEOs see themselves and their companies as dominating their environment. Being a dominant force in a dominant company, these CEOs expected employees to execute their personal vision, with not a lot of discussion.

Bad Habit #2: Failed CEOs identify so completely with their company that there is no clear boundary between their personal interests and their corporation's interests. They begin to think of the company as 'their' company. Being the CEO of a sizable corporation today is probably the closest thing to being king of your own country. This leads to unilateral decision-making.

Bad Habit #3: They think they have all the answers. Apparently, the CEO of Rubbermaid thought he had a better grasp of everything than any of his direct reports, so he didn't ask for advice very often. The company went from being Fortune's Most Admired Company in America in 1993 to being acquired by the Newell conglomerate a few years later. In general, failed CEOs don't ask for advice frequently enough because they think they have the answers.

Bad Habit #4: They ruthlessly eliminate anyone who isn't completely behind them. These CEOs think their job is to instill their vision throughout the company and get everyone to buy into it. Anyone who doesn't fall in line gets eliminated. This certainly shows authoritarian dominance and top-down decision-making.

Bad Habit #5: They are consummate spokespersons, obsessed with the company's image. These CEOs are more concerned with public perceptions than with the actual facts inside the company. Instead of treating their financial accounts as an internal control tool, they treat them as a public relations tool. The creative accounting that was apparently practiced by such executives as Enron's Jeffrey Skilling or Tyco's Dennis Kozlowski was to promote the given company's image, and thereby increase company stock valuations. The trouble is that they ended up deceiving shareholders in their exuberance. Being obsessed with company image prevents honest assessment of the brutal facts of how things are actually going in a company.

Bad Habit #6: They underestimate obstacles. These failed CEOs are more concerned with 'face' than being right. They have a hard time admitting that a change of plans is needed. For example, when Webvan's core business was racking up huge losses, CEO George Shaheen was busy expanding those operations at an excessive rate, rather than seeking counsel from objective observers. That's also why leaders at Iridium and Motorola (MMI) kept investing billions of dollars to launch satellites even after it had become apparent that land-based cell phones were a better alternative. Failed CEOs do not properly estimate the magnitude of the hurdles in front of them.

Bad Habit #7: They stubbornly rely on what worked for them in the past. They use their positions of power to direct the company to do things that had worked in the past, regardless of new market conditions.

If you view these habits through the lens of organizational intelligence, you will see that each of these bad habits reduces the opportunities to use collective intelligence to solve problems.

So, the two scholarly publications: 1) *"Organizational Crisis: The Logic of Failure,"* by Gilbert Probst and Sebastian Raisch (2005), 2) *Why Smart Executives Fail*, by Sydney Finkelstein, (2003) come to the same conclusion: giving charismatic, egotistical CEOs unchecked power more often than not leads to business failure. Having a charismatic, unusually powerful CEO diminishes the use of collective intelligence. If these collapsed corporations had done a better job of sharing responsibilities, sharing information broadly, and making strategic decisions only after deliberations with a range of senior executives, these corporate disasters probably would have been avoided… or at least delayed.

CHAPTER 5: FOREVER YOUNG: AVOIDING AND REVERSING CORPORATE AGING

Regarding the question 'What can companies do to increase their chances of success and long-term survival?', we can see that having an exceptionally charismatic and powerful CEO has risks that outweigh the benefits, on average. Of course, there are exceptions, and it is possible to have both long-term survival and charismatic leadership, and the secret to mitigating the risks of charismatic leadership is to make certain that leadership uses collective intelligence, which we will be covering in more detail later.

Corporate infrastructure and culture play a large role in long-term survival. In *The Innovator's Dilemma* (1997) Christensen pointed out that the celebrated principle of "listening to your customers" is not at all helpful in avoiding disruption by a new technology. Christensen studied the disk drive industry between 1977 and 1994 and found five waves of technology advances that caused the demise of multibillion-dollar corporations and the ascendancy of others. In each case, the disrupted companies saw the new technologies coming and had examples in their laboratories. Nonetheless, new companies using the new technology drove the incumbents out of business.

There may be several reasons: perhaps the small-company advantage accrues from the fact that employees in smaller organizations are acting after thoughtful deliberation rather than following standard procedures to get their work done. Another factor might be that the infrastructure developed by a startup would be better optimized for its narrow market than that of a large company serving other markets. Or, perhaps, in a startup, power and information are spread broadly. The founders will often sweep the floor, greet customers, make coffee, check inventory, watch closely how resources are spent, and so on. But everybody else also engages in cross functional activities. Simply put, young organizations are flat, their knowledge is widely shared, the power to act is broadly distributed, the urge to innovate is constantly there, and a sense of urgency prevails. Note that this increases the availability of collective intelligence, and hence leads to better decision-making.

But couldn't a large company simply set up a new division and let it develop its own unique infrastructure and organizational genes? It depends on the degree of autonomy. Large companies historically have not done well setting up new divisions to pursue new markets. This is true even when the parent company tries to make them completely free so that they can develop their own unique organizational culture, procedures, and cost structures. An exception would be Hewlett-Packard which set up TWO entirely new divisions, one to focus on laser printers, and the other to focus on inkjet printing. Having to new and separate divisions was a big success.

In contrast, IBM set up a new PC division - in Boca Raton, Florida far away from IBM's mainframe business - to enter the PC market. As we know, this did not end well for IBM. IBM certainly had the resources to completely dominate the workstation market, the desktop computing market, and even the laptop market. And then there is Xerox. Xerox PARC invented ethernet, laser printing, object-oriented programming, scalable type fonts, and the desktop metaphor which gave rise to the "Windows" operating system and so on. Yet Xerox never became a dominant player in commercializing any of these things.

Trying to understand big company declines today has something in common with trying to understand disease 100 years ago. About 100 years ago people thought malaria was carried on swamp air. When you know about bacteria and viruses, you can imagine the right answers. But before these microorganisms were discovered, no one could have guessed that the infections they believed were passed through the air could have anything in common with reused bed linen during childbirth. The same is true of business declines. This time the invisible factor is carried on bits and bytes and is derived from organizational intelligence.

The press/media and business textbooks are not generally aware that anything so ethereal as organizational intelligence and culture may hold answers that could prevent declines and disruptions. Remember, the purpose of intelligence is to protect the survival of the host organization. Apparently, intelligence is healthier in younger organizations, and declines over time. It is easy to believe that this decline has to do with the seemingly inexorable migration of decision-making power from the many to the few, i.e., the centralization of power. This is accompanied by the introduction of rules and regulations, and the proceduralization of knowledge in corporations (and many national economies). Most organizational practices that reduce the number of actively involved human minds reduce the potential power of organizational intelligence. Is it inevitable that this regression of intelligence happens in mature companies? Probably not, as we shall see in Chapter 6.

Corporate organizational intelligence is the output of a company's employees interacting through the total set of rules, regulations, procedures, friendships, informal networks, formal networks, and connections to suppliers and customers that grow over time to accomplish the objectives of the firm. Is it possible to change the genes of a company after it is established to allow organizational intelligence to flower? Is it possible to take a mediocre or failing company and turn it into a great company? Is it possible to avoid disruption, to disrupt from within?

In Chapter 4 we noted that Stanford professor Jim Collins, in his 1994 book Built to Last, described ways to design companies for enduring greatness; to outperform the market as long as the sound business practices instituted at the beginning were indeed continued throughout the life of the firm. We saw that enduring greatness was not being achieved by the firms mentioned by Collins, and this brings into question the book's conclusions about the practices that should lead to greatness. On the other hand, Jim Collins' second book, Good to Great, is a masterpiece. It did indeed reveal principles that declining companies could use to reverse the downward trend.

5.1 Good to Great Companies

When it was published in 2001, *Good to Great* was a phenomenon. It quickly rose to the top of the charts and spent many years on bestseller lists, selling several million copies. It is probably one of the most popular business books ever written. The book was inspired by the question 'Can a mature mediocre company become a great company?' In other words, 'Can any company that is past its prime, and in the declining phase of its lifecycle, change its downward trajectory into an upward one, and if so, how?'

Jim Collins asked if there were companies that trended down for 15 years and then trended up for 15 years, showing that there was indeed a fundamental change responsible for the turnaround. Collins and his team were only able to find 11 companies (out of 1,435 followed over a 30-year period) that had turned themselves around sufficiently to be called 'great' stock performers. (The 11 companies are: Abbot, Circuit City, Fannie Mae, Gillette, Kimberly-Clark, Kroger, Nucor, Phillip Morris, Pitney Bowes, Walgreens, and Wells Fargo.) What an amazing set of companies these turned out to be! A single dollar invested in a portfolio of the 11 companies at the beginning of the 35-year study, namely 1965, would have grown to $471 by the year 2000. An equivalent amount invested in the general market would have grown to just $56. In other words, if you invested in these 11 companies just before the inflection points in the share prices, you would have beat the darlings of Wall Street, including GE, Microsoft, Coke, Intel, etc.

To provide a baseline for comparisons with these 11 remarkable companies, Collins and his students identified 11 other direct comparison companies in the same industries. This was done to rule out the possibility that the companies just happened to be in high-growth industries. An equivalent amount invested in the direct comparison companies would have grown only to $93 (compared to $471). It follows that something happened in those 11 companies that is truly extraordinary.

It's pretty clear that Jim Collins and his team understood the amazing opportunity they had before them. If they could find an answer to their research question, it would possibly reveal how to make any company great, regardless of its initial condition. They spent more than five years and 15,000 hours poring over books, newspapers, and magazine articles augmented by personal interviews with executives from the companies. They covered more than 6,000 articles and dozens of books. All this time and energy was required because nothing obvious was leaping out of their research that even remotely explained the amazing growth. Nothing was obvious about the reasons for the turnaround. A radically new rationalization of causality was needed. But before we focus on radically new answers, look at all the obvious things that were evaluated! These are exactly the things that you would think would turn a business around, if you were well-trained in modern management theories:

1. Hypothesis: A charismatic CEO from the outside came in with new ideas. In fact, the Good to Great (G2G) companies simply promoted CEOs from the inside (in 10 of 11 cases).
2. Hypothesis: The CEO was paid more and therefore tried harder. In fact, the G2G companies showed no correlation between executive compensation and success.
3. Hypothesis: The G2G companies spent more time in strategic planning. In fact, the G2G companies did not change their strategic planning practices nor spend more time planning than other companies.
4. Hypothesis: The G2G companies consciously, explicitly focused on what to do to become great. In fact, the G2G companies did nothing to explicitly pursue greatness. They largely considered what to do, what not to do, and what to stop doing . . . the immediate mechanical operations of running a business.
5. Hypothesis: New technology was invented, licensed, or otherwise utilized to initiate the transformation from mediocrity to great performance. In fact, the transformations in the G2G companies were never ignited by technology.

6. Hypothesis: A merger or acquisition took place that brought new vitality or company culture. In fact, mergers and acquisitions played no role.
7. Hypothesis: New management practices were adopted, aimed at change to management or motivating people. In fact, the G2G companies had no such "people management" off-sites, programs, or practices at the time of the turnaround.
8. Hypothesis: The G2G companies were aware at the time the transformation took place that something special happened. In fact, the G2G companies did not initiate new programs or do anything else that gave a hint that they were about to "become great."
9. Hypothesis: The G2G companies just happened to be in new-growth industries at the right time. In fact, the G2G companies were, more often than not, in mature and declining industries. (Collins, 2001)

Let's review the setting. The Collins team had identified 11 remarkable companies, companies that had been declining for at least 15 years and then suddenly changed to become the best-performing stocks in the world. What was most noteworthy and incontestable was that in every case, a new CEO took over just before these remarkable changes. The mystery was that there were no other obvious changes or new appearances of special characteristics or events in these companies. And the team looked hard for distinguishing characteristics. Nonetheless, they were not able to find a new technology, or a new management philosophy, or a new vision, or acquisitions or divestitures. The mystery deepened still further when they discovered that the new CEOs did not appear to have charisma or traditional leadership skills. Jim Collins noted the general opinion is that CEOs should be charismatic, have a vision, and then lead the organization in the direction of his vision. But the new CEOs in these 11 remarkable companies appeared to be deficient in these qualities! In fact, because of their lack of charisma, these CEOs were generally not covered by the press; and learning about them generally required interviews with employees in the companies.

Collins and his team didn't know how to make sense of this and the best they could do was to call these individuals 'Level V Leaders' (Level 5 Leaders). They wanted some acknowledgment that these leaders were superior, and they created a progression of management skills going from one to five. The only other clearly common features in the 11 companies, besides getting new CEOs, was that there was a shuffling in the ranks of senior management, and the companies seemed to spend extra effort gathering and reviewing the facts of their circumstances before taking action.

Collins has a gift for inventing memorable stories and names to communicate his ideas. Let's look at how he expresses his ideas in the book, Good to Great. You'll enjoy the language. The book has nine chapters. However, the core ideas are captured in Chapters 2, 3, and 4:

Ch. 2: Level V Leadership

1. To quote Jim Collins: "We were surprised, shocked really, to discover the type of leadership required for turning a good company into a great one. Compared to high profile leaders with big personalities who make headlines and become celebrities, the G2G leaders seem to have come from Mars. Self-effacing, quiet, reserved, even shy—these leaders are a paradoxical blend of personal humility and professional will. They are more like Lincoln and Socrates than Patton or Caesar" (2001, 13).

   Ch. 3: The "First Who . . . Then What" Principle

2. We expected that good to great leaders would begin by setting a new vision and strategy. We found instead that they first got the right people on the bus, the wrong people off the bus, and the right people in the right seats—and then they figured out where to drive it" (2001, 13).

   Ch. 4: Confront the Brutal Facts (the Stockdale Paradox)

3. "We learned that a former prisoner of war had more to teach us about what it takes to find a path to greatness than most books on corporate strategy. Every G2G company embraced what we came to call the Stockdale Paradox. You must maintain unwavering faith that you can and will prevail in the end, regardless of the difficulties. And at the same time have the discipline to confront the most brutal facts of your current reality, whatever they may be" (2001, 13).

Jim Collins had no concept of organizational or collective intelligence. However, the lessons abstracted from the chapters just mentioned could be taken as core pillars of organizational intelligence. The quoted material is from Jim Collins; the rest is my synthesis of his ideas.

1. "Level V Leadership": The only leaders that have turned major corporations around from poor performance to great performance are humble leaders, i.e., they get groups of people involved in planning and decision-making.
2. "First Who . . . Then What": Get the right people in the right seats managerially before deciding where to drive the bus. In other words, leaders should not be so presumptuous that they know the road to success without asking others to help.

3. "Confront the Brutal Facts (the Stockdale Paradox)": be brutally honest, not optimistic. In other words, gather facts and evaluate them honestly without undue optimism.

The radical new business idea that Jim Collins stumbled onto in Good to Great is that corporate governance by deliberative information-sharing completely blows away governance by charismatic leadership. Humble people ask other people for their opinions, and this increases "organizational intelligence," and organizational intelligence was the real force that created the extraordinary success of the Good to Great companies.

Collins discovered that leadership by humble, quiet, self-effacing, shy people was essential in transformations from good to great. This sort of leadership was perfect for eliciting collective intelligence from management teams. Ask yourself if you would rather attempt to offer advice to the overtly 'smartest guy in the room' or to someone humble and quiet, looking for answers. Would you feel more comfortable chatting with someone who has a habit of demonstrating his superior insight? Or someone who is genuinely curious and interested in what you have to say? In addition to the personalities of Level V leaders that encourage employees to volunteer their opinions, we have the other two principal findings in *Good to Great:* "first who . . . then what" (2001, 41), (get comfortable communicators), and the Stockdale Paradox (get the objective truth). These are also precisely the tactics that promote group decision-making. They are quite similar to what Ricardo Semler did when revitalizing Semco. In other words, to exploit group decision-making, you would not want CEOs with strongly held ideas, visions, prejudices, and agendas. You would want the kind of managers who can exploit group intelligence by sitting down with an open mind to gather facts before taking action. And you would want senior managers to hear all the facts, and not have bad news excluded or good news exaggerated as is typically offered in a misguided attempt to inspire team enthusiasm.

In short, you want the lessons of the "Stockdale Paradox" and "first who ...then what" to determine who can contribute information, then learn to drive the bus, and finally acquire Level V leaders, humble leaders who listen to advice.

Corporate organizational intelligence depends on people. How to get more people involved in decision-making? Clearly not everyone can be involved in the decision-making required at all levels. The CEO should not be deciding if an employee over-spent his expense account, or where the janitor puts his brooms. The janitor should not be deciding resource allocation between marketing and R&D. So, how can information and power to act get optimally distributed? Consider Amazon and Semco.

5.2 Southwest Airlines: Showcasing Company Culture

Another remarkable business success that shows the power of organizational intelligence is Southwest Airlines. As one indicator of success, Southwest Airlines stock appreciated more from the early 1970s into the early 2000s than any other publicly traded stock in the US. It has been profitable every year, for 35 years, since it went public. And it achieved this remarkable growth in one of the most competitive and troubled industries in the world. Most other US airlines suffered declining profitability, bankruptcies, and mergers during the same time period. As of 2005, five of the ten largest airlines had filed for bankruptcy. Northwest Airlines, United Airlines, and Delta Airlines had all been in business at least 35 years when Southwest Airlines was founded. Yet, in 2005, Southwest had grown to have a market capitalization four times the others combined.

Southwest Airlines was founded in 1967, by Herb Kelleher and Rollin King in Dallas, Texas. For the first five years of its existence, it was a tiny airline with only three aircraft and only served three cities within Texas (Houston, Austin, and Dallas). But Herb Kelleher had a vision of Southwest being able to make air travel so convenient and inexpensive people would prefer to fly rather than drive for out-of-town trips. He focused on driving costs down, while also improving convenience and customer care.

He and his team identified at least a half dozen tricks to drive costs down, including:

1. Shorter turnarounds at terminals (10-20 minutes vs. the 60-minute industry average. This includes unloading and boarding new passengers, refueling, restocking refreshments, cleaning the plane . . . all within a 10-minute window.)
2. Using only one type of aircraft. They used only Boeing 737s for many years to lower training, maintenance, and inventory costs.
3. Avoiding cities with congested terminals.
4. Making ticketing easier by offering open seating.

5. Trusting employees rather than saddling them with rules and regulations. The President Southwest stated in a public interview that its employees come first, customers second, and shareholders third.

All this has certainly helped Southwest, but the real secret of their success isn't captured by these cost-containment tactics. The real secret is in their corporate culture.

The company culture may have evolved over time but during its first 30 years of operation and extraordinary stock market performance, it included unusual trust the company put in its employees, which includes giving ordinary employees the authority to make decisions that would normally be reserved for upper management. When situations arise allowing employees to make on-the-spot decisions, they are encouraged to do so, as long as there is no conflict of interest.

Employees are constantly educated and informed to better understand the company, its mission, its customers, and its competition. Since inception, Southwest has cultivated a remarkable culture that embraced everyone in the company and treated them as one big family. It has been said that Herb Kelleher knew everyone by name even when the company had grown to more than 1,000 employees.

The company has had a practice of celebrating successes and special occasions including anniversaries, Halloween, Christmas, chili cook-offs, and practically any other excuse to have a gathering. Furthermore, Southwest's care for its employees extends beyond social gatherings. Its employees are allowed to fly free anywhere their planes go. Not only do employees themselves fly free, but so do spouses, eligible dependent children, and parents of employees, as long as space is available. Profit-sharing is also provided to all employees when the company meets its profitability goals set each year. A generous stock purchase plan allows employees to share in the success of the company. Through the plan, employees pay only 90% of market value for the stock. In addition, employees are also given the benefit of medical, dental, vision, and life insurance coverage. And layoffs are essentially unheard of.

This sort of culture promotes extraordinary productivity (the highest productivity rates in the industry and the lowest employee turnover rates in the airline industry, circa 6.5% per year) as noted by REF. In addition, the company now serves almost twice as many customers annually as any other airline in the US (as of the early 21st century, when our data were being collected).

So, to sum up, Southwest Airlines truly has enjoyed extraordinary stock performance, growth, efficiencies, employee satisfaction; and these apparently come more from its culture than anything else, at least according to its founder.

Herb Kelleher once said on a TV interview with CBS 60 Minutes that there is no great secret to what Southwest does (60minutes, 1989). He said, "The company's operations are there for the world to see. Competitors can go to Boeing and buy an airplane, rent space in an airport, and otherwise reproduce the Southwest Airlines model. However, the real asset and value of Southwest is its people, and that cannot be so easily copied." (I may not have gotten the words exactly right, but this was certainly the spirit of voice said.)

This may take a moment to sink in. So, let me state it again. The critical factor that allowed this company to outperform all other companies in its industry, and indeed create the best-performing stock in the US for a 35-year period, is its people, a.k.a. corporate culture, according to its co-founder, Herb Kelleher. Corporate culture provides the scaffolding on which organizational intelligence grows. Remember that two of the fundamental tenets of organizational intelligence are decentralization of decision-making and minimization of rules and regulations. Southwest Airlines certainly did this. Southwest also created a sense of employee extended family with the spirit of taking care of each other, which helps enormously with motivation and goodwill.

5.3 Microsoft: Level V Leadership and Timing

As the world knows, Bill Gates (and co-founder Paul Allen) founded Microsoft in 1976, and Microsoft stock made Bill Gates the world's richest man (briefly) about 30 years later. The company didn't go public until March 1986. But you can see from graphs of Microsoft's share price that it was lackluster and flat for the first 10 years. Then it enjoyed a short run up for five years along with all tech stocks because of the birth of the internet. After the crash of the internet bubble in the year 2000, Microsoft stock was truly flat for almost 15 years. Being flat is consistent with the predictions of the yearbook *Creative Destruction* by Richard Foster and Sarah Kaplan of McKinsey and Company, which said that no company outperforms the market for more than 15 years.

But then, something happened in 2014 that caused the company to surge upwards in the market again. That remarkable thing was Satya Nadella. Satya Nadella joined Microsoft in 1992 and took over the reins as CEO of Microsoft in 2014. He turned out to be a Level V leader, as defined in Chapter 5.1 in the description of the Good to Great companies. As you can see from the plot, the market capitalization for Microsoft went from $400 billion to $1.5 trillion in the five years after he took over. Similarly, the share price started going up dramatically when Satya became CEO in 2014.

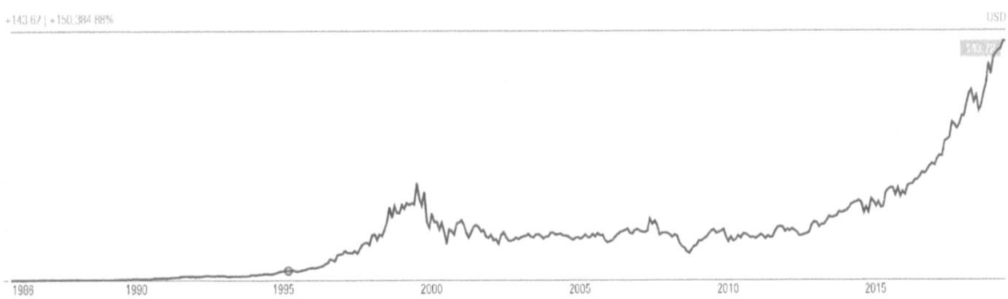

Figure 10: *Microsoft share price from 1996 to 2021*

Source: ***MorningStar, 2021***

Some of the stock appreciation was undoubtedly a result of the company buying back its own stock on public markets (so-called company buybacks), but the more significant development was the cultural shift that came with Satya. So, what might make Satya a Level V leader? Level V leaders, according to Jim Collins, were quiet insiders and their demeanor was distinctly humble. In watching some of the many YouTube videos of interviews with Satya, you can see him crediting his father and mother for instilling in him a sense of confidence and humility. Satya is certainly an insider, and he is certainly humble as well, judging from his interviews. When asked about the secrets of good management, he says "I think it is to ascribe more power to others than to ourselves" (Nadella, 2019).

Probably the most important part of Satya's Level V leadership style is his support of empathetic collaboration. He famously is quoted as saying, "when you join Microsoft it's not to be cool, but to make others cool," (Nadella, 2019) or in other words, your job is to help others be successful. He also elevates the role of empathy. He wrote in an email to Microsoft employees that "[our job] requires us to truly understand and share the feelings of another person" (Nadella, 2017). This is exactly what we just learned that IDEO ascribes as its most fundamental guiding principle. These things are accelerators for collective/organizational intelligence and demonstrate the power of empathy and humility as genes of organizational intelligence.

5.4 Spinoffs, Crowdsourcing, Outsourcing and Contracting

We have just seen how several corporate cultures promoted growth and delayed the onset of corporate decline. There are three other organizational tactics that can help organizational intelligence grow: outsourcing, crowdsourcing, and independent business units.

Outsourcing:

There is another way large companies can be revitalized: outsourcing. If large companies are bogged down by bureaucracy (e.g., too many rules and regulations, hierarchies, and centralized control), might not the problems be at least partially remedied through outsourcing?

Outsourcing and contracting have become widely practiced and are the norm these days for large industrial companies. Take Ford, General Motors, or Toyota for example. Each of these companies has on the order of 1,000 contractors that deliver components that get assembled into finished cars. Of course, when these companies were founded, they did not start out with multitudes of contractors. They were vertically integrated, meaning that they did everything in-house. In the case of Ford, the company not only made its own tires, but it also owned rubber plantations that produced rubber for tires, mining rights to produce steel for their cars, glass production facilities for windows, and so on. These days the big car companies purchase tires, steel, and windows from independent providers.

They probably would face antitrust laws if they attempted to vertically integrate today, but the more important fact is that they would not want to, even if they could, because it's more efficient and less costly for these big firms to use contractors. In other words, breaking up a manufacturing process into stages and outsourcing the stages reduces costs! It reduces costs because contractors are smaller organizations with the freedom to develop their own internal cost structures.

This is explained nicely by John Seely Brown, formerly CEO of PARC in a talk he gave circa 2005. The story takes place in Chongqing, China, where there was both a Honda-owned motorbike manufacturing facility and a state-owned motorbike manufacturing plant. A number of mom-and-pop shops started offering supplies to these factories. After a while, the small shops shared information between themselves and figured out how to redesign the motorbikes to reduce manufacturing costs and improve performance. Rather than try to convince the factories to change, the small shops just started manufacturing motorbikes by themselves as a federation of suppliers and final assemblers. They quickly started out-selling Honda in its biggest market, Vietnam, and then gradually started selling to the rest of the world. At this point more than half of the motorbikes manufactured worldwide come from the Chongqing area. The collective intelligence of the initial shop-owned motorbike suppliers was high because the suppliers were all talking to each other, peer to peer, with no central authority attempting to orchestrate. They were all equals. The economic incentive to share information was clear. They could make more money with their innovative lower-cost designs by working with each other and then selling directly to customers, rather than supplying Honda or the state-owned company. And Honda could not possibly compete, due to its higher overhead and lower rate of innovation.

John Seely Brown had another story about organizational intelligence (although that was not his subject). The story was about the way General Motors was finding its subcontractors and how it differed from the way Toyota was finding its subcontractors. The standard practice for most of the last 50 years, in Detroit, GM would put out a design document and request bids from potential suppliers. GM would do this regularly after each contract was finished. The intention was to select the lowest cost bidder from a pool of potential suppliers. The result was that suppliers would not share any inventions they made with GM for fear that GM would share them with their competitors. This was in stark contrast to the way Toyota would select its subcontractors in Japan. Instead, competing vendors would accept a visit from Toyota engineers, who would simply walk around and make their own assessments of the likely efficiencies and costs from the vendor. They would then select a vendor and then make the vendor a partner by guaranteeing contract renewals year after year, unless there was an egregious failure on the part of the vendor. In this situation, the subcontractors generally shared innovations with Toyota, and even other contractors, because they knew their positions would not be threatened by competition.

Crowdsourcing:

An even more cost-effective way of getting intellectual work done is crowdsourcing. Most jobs are not suited to crowdsourcing, but those which are served remarkably well. In the late 1990s, Goldcorp Inc. was a Toronto-based gold mining firm that had been mining for 50 years in Red Lake, Ontario. They had run out of known deposits and were gradually going out of business.

Rob McEwen, the CEO of Goldcorp, attended an MIT conference for Young Presidents in 1999 during which he learned about how Linus Torvalds had spearheaded the development of the world's most powerful operating system, 'open-sourced' Linux, by sharing source code with everyone in the world and allowing anyone to suggest modifications to the code.

McEwen consequently decided to share the geological survey maps gathered by the company on the internet with all the data the company had gathered for the past 50 years. The company had highly paid geologists. In fact, they had just spent $10 million updating their survey maps. Geological survey maps are generally considered to be a major intellectual asset and a guarded secret. The in-house company geologists were skeptical that anyone could do a better job than they had in estimating where gold deposits were to be found. Nonetheless, McEwen forged ahead. In March 2000, Goldcorp began advertising a $575,000 pool of prize money available to be shared with anyone/everyone that could contribute to reasonable estimates of where gold could be found. The land where they had mining rights was a 55,000-acre property shown on the Goldcorp website. Eventually, more than 1,000 virtual prospectors from 50 countries analyzed the data and returned estimates to Goldcorp. The estimates came from geologists, graduate students, consultants, mathematicians, and military officers. The contestants had identified 110 targets on the Red Lake property, 50% of which had not been previously identified by the company. Over 80% of the new targets had substantial quantities of gold. In fact, the web-based community identified locations where 8,000,000 ounces of gold have been subsequently mined. When the price of gold was around $1,500 an ounce, this amounted to $12 billion. That's a remarkable return on investment of approximately half a million dollars. The company subsequently grew from $100 million annually into a $9 billion success with a corresponding spectacular increase in share value for the company (for further on Goldcorp see Tapscott and Williams, 2006, Chapter One).

This success did not go unnoticed. In fact, it ushered in an era of crowdsourcing and XPRIZE competitions. For example, Procter & Gamble's CEO, A.G. Lafley, decreed that the company should try to source 50% of its new product ideas from outside the company, starting around the year 2000. XPRIZEs are multimillion-dollar prizes in which a sponsor donates the prize money and invites any and all companies to attempt to achieve the objectives set forth in the competition. Peter Diamendis conceived the first one, which was for the first non-government organization to launch a reusable crewed spacecraft into space twice within two weeks. The price was $10 million, and it was won in 2004 by SpaceShipOne, financed by

Microsoft co-founder Paul Allen. It is claimed by the XPRIZE foundation that this process is approximately 10 times more efficient than in-house development of the same products or technologies.

As another example, crowdsourced espionage intelligence gathering has been shown to outperform CIA operatives in target countries in predicting international political outcomes, according to the *Good Judgment Project* sponsored by the CIA. They solicited opinions from approximately 3,000 people in the project, people who were laymen, not professional forecasters or subject matter experts; their main research tool was Google. However, a technique named CHAMP[5] was developed and it seemed to help prediction accuracy. Even without CHAMP, by combining the crowdsourced inputs, the CIA obtained forecasts of international unrest that were 30% better than intelligence officers with access to classified information. With CHAMP, they did a little better.

If crowdsourced intelligence from large groups of people works so well in answering questions for the CIA, how about applying crowdsourced intelligence for other national domestic needs such as uncovering potential terrorism? The Defense Advanced Research Projects Agency (DARPA) was/is interested in trying out crowdsourced intelligence techniques. So, they conceived of a competition and called it The Red Balloon Challenge. It was announced on October 29, 2009, and offered a $40,000 prize to the first group to accurately locate ten balloons DARPA would place in various locations over the entirety of the USA. Organizations and individuals signed up, including universities, government R&D labs, and lots of hobbyists. They programmed open-source collaboration software and launched social media campaigns. A team from MIT Media Lab, headed by Alex Pentland (whom we met earlier in Chapter 2 & 3), apparently didn't find out about the competition until a few days before it was to formally launch. So, they invented an extraordinarily simple and clever approach.

Instead of building software systems to scour social media and satellite data, they built a website that stated approximately: When you sign up to join the MIT Red Balloon Challenge Team, you'll be provided with a personalized invitation link, http://balloon.mit.edu/... which you can use to register yourself as well as forward to all your friends, so all your friends sign up too. If anyone you invite, or anyone they invite, or anyone they invite, etc. wins money, so will you! We're giving $2,000 per balloon to the first person to send us the correct coordinates, and we're also giving $,1000 to the person who invited them. Then we're giving $500 to whoever invited the inviter, and $250 to whoever invited them, and so on.

---

[5]"CHAMP" stands for Comparisons, Historical trends,
Average opinions, Mathematical models, and Predictable biases.

At 10:00 a.m. Eastern Time on December 5, 2009, DARPA stationed the 10 balloons in secret locations ranging from Union Square in downtown San Francisco to a park in Delaware to a baseball field in Houston, Texas. DARPA expected it to take several weeks before any organization would be able to find all 10 balloons. Thousands of teams swung into action, including people who had received the MIT announcement a couple of days earlier with the invitation to use the MIT website. It took MIT only 8 hours and 50 minutes to announce they had found all ten balloons. It turned out that 4,665 people had participated. How did they do it? The answer about why the MIT team won, besides their incredibly clever method of dividing prize money among participants, is the fact that they shared the prize money at all. By sharing financial gains with other people, they produced extraordinary collaboration. Of course, the creation of a platform to share information was also a critical piece of the puzzle.

Organizations that want to exploit the wisdom of crowds, and use crowdsourced assistance in solving problems, should focus on simple problem statements that can be easily understood, with unambiguous metrics for payment, and some reasonable compensation scheme. For the moment, simply note that crowdsourcing and XPRIZEs can be potential contributors to organizational intelligence. And they can certainly reduce costs when they can be utilized. But there is more to the story that unfolds below.

Independent business units and spinoffs:

Independent business units behave more like startups than big corporations, i.e., they exhibit a higher level of organizational intelligence per employee. Illinois Tool Works (ITW) provides an example. This is a firm with a $14 billion USD annual income, with 45,000 employees, and has been growing for nearly 100 years. Its share price for the last decade increased 354%, compared to the S&P's 206% (ITW, 2012). These are spectacular results, but its product line is pedestrian, including fasteners, automotive components, cooking equipment, and other specialty consumer items. Its magic sauce for success has two components: to create entirely independent business units for successful product lines, and to emphasize innovation constantly in all business units. When it comes to innovation, they are especially remarkable: the company has nearly 18,000 patents, which puts it among the top 100 organizations in the country for patent issuance. Currently, the firm is composed of approximately 400 business units. On average, when the business unit revenues pass $50 million, the business unit is divided into two or more new business units. The goal is to keep the business units small enough to foster an entrepreneurial management style. Having completely independent business units reduces the inefficiencies of hierarchies found in larger corporations.

CHAPTER 6: ORGANIZATIONAL INTELLIGENCE IN STARTUPS

A rank startup can often beat a business unit inside an established company, even though established companies can provide financing and subsidized services to their business units. We will now look at two spectacularly successful examples. These business units were spun out from large mature companies that were languishing inside the parent company. These examples showcase the advantages of doing away with hierarchy on the intelligence of organizations.

6.1 Springfield Remanufacturing Corporation

The Springfield Remanufacturing Corporation story is a David and Goliath story in which a small spinoff company succeeded where the giant parent company was failing.

The story begins with the giant International Harvester, a company founded in 1902. By the 1980s it was a huge multibillion-dollar operation with 17 factories throughout America producing tractors and trucks and other farm equipment. The country was going into a minor recession and the company had taken on $6 billion of debt and was hemorrhaging cash. The company had an old-style hierarchical, slightly confrontational management, and they were unable to innovate rapidly enough. They laid off about a thousand people a week over a two-year period. They eventually decided to close down nonprofitable factories and sell assets, including one in Springfield, Missouri. So, in 1979 they sent Jack Stack to Springfield to close down the factory gracefully over a two-year period of time.

But Jack fell in love with the people working there. They were hard-working, honest, inventive, and optimistic. Jack worked with them, attempting to turn the situation around so International Harvester wouldn't close them down. Finally, Jack decided that the best way to secure their future would be to buy the factory from International Harvester. As an expert in quality control and how to measure and record everything in factories, Jack was astonished to discover that all that the banks cared about were the financial statements, profit and loss, balance sheet and cash flow statements. Jack didn't know anything about these kinds of metrics, so he learned them, and then he took his cash flow and income statements and went to 54 different lending institutions. He was turned down by them all. But in the process, he had an epiphany about what it took to run a company. He realized that it's wrong to hide company financials from employees and that every employee had the right to know all the details that financials reveal about how a company is doing.

He said in an interview that he made a promise to God that if he ever got the funding, he would share all this information with all employees. He said that he knew he could appeal to a higher level of intelligence in the people by sharing this information with them (Stack, 2014). Finally, he was able to borrow $8.9 million to purchase the company from International Harvester, along with 13 other employees who put in $100,000 of their own money.

By 1988, five years later, the business had a value of $43 million. And its spectacular growth has continued. The company's secret sauce is trusting the intelligence of the people in the company to understand the company financials and act in their own best interest. The company is now known as SRC Holdings Corporation and has founded and financed 60 companies in the last 37 years. It remains a 100% employee-owned company employing over 1,600 people, with sales of over $450 million. Even though it is not publicly traded, the company grants shares to its employees. They claim the share price went from $0.10 per share to about $200 a share as of 2015. They say that for the founders this was an increase of 292,000% in its stock value since 1983. Since 2010 through 2019, SRC has experienced an average of 16% year-over-year stock growth (The Great Game of Business Inc., 2018).

The secret of their success begins with sharing financial information. In addition, they vigorously support ongoing business education for all employees, provided free throughout the company. Jack's promise to God was to make sure everyone understands the company's financials. He delivers on that by making certain that company financials are published widely (e.g., in lunchrooms and the factory floor) and showcased in weekly meetings. They've coined the term "open-book management" to describe what they do (The Great Game of Business, 2019). But their company culture doesn't stop with sharing financial information—they try every way possible to make all employees feel as team members and partners. It is noteworthy that they refer to themselves as associates, not employees. The company puts its employees first, ahead of customers. They attempt to create the feeling that the company cares about their future with bonus programs, health insurance training programs, tuition refund programs, Employee Stock Ownership Plans, and a company 401k match contribution. In addition, Stack has attempted to make tracking financial numbers fun by turning it into a game, which he calls the great game of business, with teams competing against other teams.

Jack Stack himself has authored two books on the subject, *The Great Game of Business: The Only Sensible Way to Run a Company* (2013), and *A Stake in the Outcome* (2002).

In addition, SRC Holdings has set up a division called The Great Game of Business to share their theory of business. The company says hundreds of companies have by now embraced the principles of open-book management and the practices advocated by The Great Game of Business and have achieved outstanding results.

According to The Great Game of Business, a study conducted on 15 years of data concluded that companies who fully implemented the open book management practices of The Great Game of Business consistently experienced remarkable growth, profitability, and employee engagement, including;

1. Revenue Growth (24% CAGR) *
2. Profit Growth (88% CAGR) *

* CAGR: Compounded Annual Growth Rate

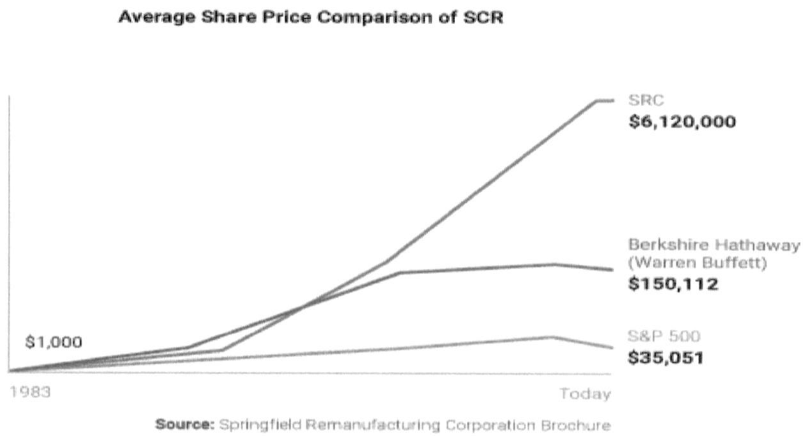

Figure 11: *Average Share Price Comparison of SRC*

Source: ***The Great Game of Business, 2018***

SRC discovered the power of openly sharing information and the power to act on it with organizational members, which are the defining characteristics of organizational intelligence. In this case the information shared was financial information along with company business plans.

"The best, most efficient, most profitable way to operate a business is to educate everybody on how the business works, give them a voice in how that the company is run, and provide them with a stake in the financial outcome, good or bad" (Stack, 2013). SRC certainly shows one way of elevating a company's organizational intelligence.

Another startup, Chobani, illustrates *another set of organizational genes* that promote businesses success.

6.2 Chobani

Chobani is another remarkable story of a great business success starting with a product that was failing in the hands of a big corporation. In this case, the very large company was Kraft Foods Inc.

In 2005 Kraft Foods Inc. was a multibillion-dollar mature corporation in slow decline. Over the years it had marketed many usually successful brands such as Maxwell House, Milka, Nabisco, Oreo, Oscar Mayer, Philadelphia, Trident, and Tang. Several of its brands annually earned more than $1 billion. Management decided to streamline operations and divest themselves of low profit businesses such as the yogurt plant in South Edmeston, New York. In his 2019 TED Talk, Hamdi Ulukaya, an immigrant from Turkey, explained that he saw a flier advertising the sale of the yogurt plant in upstate New York and decided, out of idle curiosity, to drive by the location and take a look. The plant was at the end of a dead-end road. The building was decrepit, cracking and smelled of "milk left out in the sun" (Ulukaya, 2019). The plant itself had 55 employees at that time. Their only job was to close things down, forever. Hamdi met people there who had worked at this factory their entire adult lives. Their situation was heartbreaking. These people had a sense of community. They had watched each other's kids grow up. They cared about each other but seemed powerless to stop the wheels of progress.

Hamdi explained how he imagined some CEO with a spreadsheet in some tower making decisions based on the numbers only, entirely oblivious to the human costs. He really wanted to help these people. Hamdi wasn't doing well financially. He had a small tea shop which wasn't making a lot of money and he wasn't enjoying it either. It seemed unlikely that he could possibly finance the purchase of an 85-year-old factory. Having grown up in the Kurdish Turkish mountains with cheese-making and yogurt-making in his blood, he thought he might have a chance to make it work. So, after several months of negotiating with lending organizations, he was able to purchase the plant. He immediately hired 5 of the 55 employees back and they began the process of experimenting with the production of a different kind of yogurt, a Greek yogurt, which would be called Chobani. Over the course of the next two years, Hamdi managed to hire each of the original 55 employees back, plus a couple hundred more. The factory grew and prospered, and seven years later Chobani was the best-selling yogurt in America and operated the largest yogurt factory in the world (Ulukaya, 2019).

This is an amazing story with lessons for entrepreneurs and information theorists. Culture is at the heart of this success, but not simply the yogurt culture—it was the family-oriented business culture that mattered even more. Hamdi and his dedicated team worked out corporate planning together. They became dedicated to each other and to the business that was going to keep them and their families together. Hamdi made sure they all had a financial stake in the company and would benefit from its success. Hamdi himself had a sense of service to the community that was very real and very inspiring to his factory employees. Hamdi's TED Talk went on to say that the purpose of business should not be to maximize profit for shareholders, but to take care of the employees first.

The spirit of taking care of your team or business unit shows up regularly in the genes of successful companies (recall Southwest Airlines, Semco, and SRC). Hamdi also said that businesses need to support and be involved with the communities and municipalities they are part of. This is another one of those subtle pillars of corporate success, if you recall the work of Richard Florida and Alex Pentland (see Chapter 2 & 3) that showed that innovation is a social phenomenon that benefits from diversity and the novelty of the surrounding community. The final pearl of wisdom that Hamdi gave was the need to listen to consumer feedback. That phone number Chobani put on products for customers to call to complain or ask questions . . . that number was Hamdi's personal phone number, for the first several years. The general principle obviously is that feedback from customers is invaluable.

But let's get back to the truly provocative interplay between planning, big organizations, and small organizations. All business organizations, large and small, thrive on continual learning in designing new products and services, optimizing internal processes, and defending themselves and their products against competition. Learning is always facilitated by a process of trial-and-error experimentation. It requires soliciting feedback from customers and sharing it. It requires empowering everyone to experiment, to gather information and customer feedback, to build prototypes or modify service routines, and it requires empowering people to act on any problems they encounter at whatever level they are in a company. And everyone needs to be motivated enough to take initiative. Motivation is certainly increased by a culture in which people are respected, appreciated, and feel part of a team.

These are some of the general principles. We know empirically that it becomes more difficult to apply them as companies grow larger. But there certainly are larger companies that have developed their own set of genes that influence organizational intelligence. Chapter 7 now goes on to look at what larger companies have done to develop organizational intelligence.

CHAPTER 7: ORGANIZATIONAL INTELLIGENCE FROM REMARKABLE CULTURES

We now look at five extraordinarily successful companies and notice how their cultural genes differed, but each in their own way created a basis for superior organizational intelligence and their superior success.

7 .1 Semco: The Power of Industrial Democracy

Wouldn't it be wonderful to work in a company where you are your own boss, and you could set your own schedule? Where everyone is happy and glad to come to work? Where there is a sense of community? And everyone generally feels like they are contributing to a larger cause? You may be surprised to learn that at least one company like this already exists, Semco. And it is the archetype for superior corporate organizational intelligence.

Ricardo took over a small family-owned business, Semco, in Brazil in 1980 when he was 21 years old. The family business was manufacturing marine pumps, mixers, and shakers. Within 12 years he turned Semco into one of Brazil's biggest and most successful corporations. Revenue grew from US$4 million in 1984 to $35 million by 1994 to $212 million by 2003.

But things didn't start out that way. Initially Ricardo was a traditional authoritarian manager, working incredible hours, and after a couple of years, he managed to double company revenues from $1 million to $2 million, but at great personal cost. He had an emotional breakdown because of work-related stress. He was told by his doctors that he wouldn't live to age 30 if he didn't dramatically reduce the stress in his life. He needed to change his management style if he were going to live from a traditional hierarchical management style to something more relaxed, probably relatively flat where everyone could take on more management responsibility.

So, in 1984, when Ricardo accepted the fact that he needed to change his management style at Semco, he read every book he could get his hands on which included management advice. He read Alfred Sloan's *My Years with General Motors* (1963), and Tom Peters' *In Search of Excellence* (1982). He read popular business writers such as John Naisbitt, Peter Drucker, Alvin Toffler, Robert Townsend, Kenichi Ohmae, Marvin Minsky, Henry Mintzberg, and

Ichak Adizes. He tried implementing what he thought was the best of their ideas. But nothing made much difference. He eventually gave up on business theory and decided to concentrate on corporate democracy and allowing employees to help make decisions for themselves without being told to do so by managers. And it worked. Consequently Semco enjoyed spectacular growth, and Ricardo became one of the world's most admired business innovators.

To share what he did at Semco, Ricardo wrote *Turning the Tables,* published in Brazil in 1988, in Portuguese. His book became the all-time best-selling nonfiction book in Brazil. Four years after publishing *Turning the Tables* (1993), he rewrote the book in English and published it under the name Maverick. His corporate success and fame spread over the next decade and in 2003 he wrote another updated version: *The Seven-day Weekend* (2003). Of course, Ricardo knew nothing about the concept of organizational intelligence, but he nonetheless explicitly listed techniques that ended up enhancing organizational intelligence, by sharing information and the power to act on it. One technique was that he made Semco more democratic.

To increase the level of democratic governance, he did the following:

1. Let workers set their own hours and pay scale
2. Posted salaries for all employees to see
3. Shared all company financial information openly on billboards
4. Limited all memos to one page in length
5. Allowed workers to review their supervisor's performance
6. Eliminated the traditional organization chart
7. Practiced profit sharing
8. Eliminated policy and rule manuals and instead trusted in people's judgment
9. Made business units small enough that everyone understands everything that goes on
10. Practiced job rotation

Ricardo was exceedingly open and honest in his dealings with customers and suppliers. With customers he would sometimes open his own company books and show all the expenses his internal operations incurred. He would then ask customers what they thought they should pay and ask suppliers what they should charge.

I mention these things because companies thrive when employees respect the people they're working with and for. It increases organizational intelligence. Ricardo's own words tell the story eloquently (from the introduction to his book *Maverick*):

> Every Wednesday afternoon dozens of men and women file through the front gate on their way to a third-floor meeting room at Semco, the company I lead in São Paulo, Brazil. The guard at the entrance has been expecting them. For years now, executives from some of the biggest and best-known companies in the world, IBM, General Motors, Ford, Kodak, Bayer, Nestlé, Goodyear, Firestone, Pirelli, Alcoa, BASF, Chase Manhattan, Siemens, Dow Chemical, Mercedes-Benz, and Yashica among them, have been making an unlikely pilgrimage to our nondescript industrial complex on the outskirts of the city… Semco manufactures an impressively varied roster of products, including pumps that can empty an oil tanker in the night, dishwashers capable of scrubbing 4,100 plates an hour, cooling units for air conditioners that keep huge office towers comfortable during the most sweltering of heat waves, mixers that blend everything from rocket fuel to bubble gum, and entire biscuit factories, with 6,000 separate components and 16 miles of wiring. But it's not what Semco makes that has executives and management experts the world over waiting months for a chance to tour our plants and offices. It's the way the people of Semco make it (2003, 1).

Ricardo's book goes on to explain that they have hundreds if not thousands of applications for every employment opening. It explains that the company is democratic, and that everyone gets involved in making the decisions that govern the company's future.

In his early 20s, Ricardo worked incredibly long hours, surrounding himself with hard-driving, numbers-oriented, disciplined executives. Over the next three years he managed to grow Semco to a $3 million company from the $1 million base which he had inherited from his father. Then, at the age of 24, 50 pounds overweight and exhausted, he collapsed on the factory floor of a facility he was visiting. After extensive physical examination, he was told by the doctors that he was the most stressed young man they had ever seen. He was further informed that if he didn't change his ways, he would not live to see his 30th birthday. Other than that, he was fine, with no serious heart disease or cancer. Ricardo recalled, "When I first started working at Semco, I was shocked by the oppression I found. To someone who spent much of his adolescence playing rock 'n roll, rules and procedures at some code left me numb. Still, I tried to become the embodiment of a traditional executive . . . and I succeeded. I became a tough guy" (2003, 66). And he paid a price a less-sensitive man might have avoided—he almost died from stress. It was then he knew he had to change.

In 1985, Ricardo set about trying to understand how to reduce stress in his life. He fired his most aggressive senior managers and entered into a period of corporate experimentation, introspection, and innovation, aimed at making Semco a stress-free work environment. Ricardo was quite clear that he wanted to improve his company's work environment for everyone, not just himself. Soon his ambition went beyond providing a stress-free environment. He wanted to provide an improved quality of life for everyone. He wanted Semco to be a place where employees would feel their spirits uplifted, and a place where human needs were cared for, as well as their financial needs.

Ricardo recounts the parable of three stonecutters:

> A traveler came upon three stonecutters. He asked each of them in turn what they did for a living.
>
> The first stonecutter said, 'I am paid to cut stones'…
>
> The second stonecutter said, 'I have special techniques and tools to shape stones'…
>
> The third stonecutter said, 'I build cathedrals'

Semler was determined that its employees should want to build cathedrals. But it wasn't all that clear how to do this. Ultimately, Ricardo transformed Semco management into a democracy. It didn't happen all at once, but gradually over a year or two. At first, small decisions were handed over to democratic processes. Gradually larger decisions, and more decisions, were given over to democratic processes. As more and more people got involved in making decisions, the better the decisions became, and the greater the commitment of the employees to outcomes.

Further insight can be gained into how to create firms that are eternally young by looking at some more of what Ricardo said:

1. At Semco, we practice truth with a simple formula: free sharing of information. We are so committed to it that we don't just tell people they have a right to information. We actively present it to them in e-mails and at democratic meetings. We also encourage people to learn how to use the information at their fingertips…

2. To survive in modern times, a company must have an organizational structure that accepts change as its basic premise, lets tribal customs thrive, and fosters a power that is derived from respect, not rules. In other words, the successful companies will be the ones that put quality of life first. Do this and the rest—quality of product, productivity of workers, profits for all—will follow…
3. At Semco we did away with structures that dictate the 'hows' and created fertile soil for differences. We gave people an opportunity to test, question, and disagree. We let them determine their own futures. We let them come and go as they wanted, work at home if they wished, set their own salaries, choose their own bosses. We let them change their minds and ours, prove us wrong when we are wrong, make us humbler…
4. We quickly realized that opening our books to employees meant they had to read them—and this requires quite a bit of training. The complicated accounting procedures didn't make a lot of sense to the common man. [. . .] We needed a clearer method of presenting our accounts. We realized there were only a half dozen numbers that really mattered at any of our businesses… As control wanes, creativity and shared values bloom. An army that fights for what they believe in arises from this harvest of ideas, varied practices, and close contact with the real world. Mission takes a backseat in the army jeep, and generals can relax while the soldiers and lieutenants draw up the map themselves. (2003)

Industrial Democracy

What I hope leaps out at you is the fact that Semco is a democracy. To make their democracy work, everyone at Semco has free and easy access to all company information, especially information that is usually hidden from employees in most companies. In addition, individuals are free of rules and regulations, and free to make decisions on their own in situations where most companies require a great deal of oversight, authorizations, and paperwork.

Furthermore, strategic decisions are made by groups of people, by democratic voting, rather than by smaller groups of managers. This is yet another example of exploiting the wisdom of groups, the collective mind, which makes better decisions than those of individuals. Semco demonstrates that group decision-making, using democratic principles, is not only practical, but superior to traditional management practices where bosses make the strategic decisions. The rules that implement democratic decision-making in a company are the genes for collective intelligence.

This story is particularly important because it shows that an established company can be transformed from old-style hierarchical management into a democracy, and through doing so create an environment that allows organizational intelligence to grow with all the benefits that superior intelligence brings.

7.2 Walmart: A Pioneer in Automation and Employee Engagement

At its inception in 1963, Walmart had a culture of learning and a partnership baked into its DNA by its founder, Sam Walmart. Sam was fanatical about wanting employees and managers to feel that they were partners and could influence management decisions. The result was that Walmart developed exceptional organizational intelligence, which enabled it – in a mere 50 years – to become the world's largest retailer.

An overarching management principle at Walmart has always been reducing costs. A side effect of this principle has been low salaries for Walmart employees. However, the other side effects have been a collection of policies and practices that have benefited humanity, enabling lower income citizens to afford a better lifestyle.

By 2013, exactly 50 years after its founding, Walmart employed 2.6 million people, more than the US Department of Defense (about 1.4 million), and the Chinese People's Liberation Army (about two million), making it the world's largest employer. Furthermore, its annual revenue was more than $500 billion, which was more than any other company on the planet. The company's annual shareholders meeting is the largest in the world. It is held in an athletic stadium (the Bud Walton Arena at the University of Arkansas) because of its size and need to accommodate the 20,000 or so people who show up. Walmart is also the largest real estate owner, and truck fleet operator in the US; and largest employer in the USA, Mexico, and Canada.

The Company's founder, Sam Walton, was apparently a humble, hard-working man, keenly aware that the people he was serving country folk and farmers who could not afford high prices. If you followed Sam Walton on a visit to a Walmart store, you would see him doing jumping jack calisthenics with store associates. He tried to convey a sense of partnership, caring, and even family to his employees. Sam visibly wanted everyone who worked for him to feel more like a partner than an employee. He instituted calling his employees 'associates' (Walmart was the first major employer to do so, although it has become wildly popular since he started it). He also gave employees stock options and reasonably good health insurance; a novelty when he started doing it.

All these things are abundantly visible. What is not visible is the learning culture that Sam Walton instilled in the company. He never tired of asking everyone he talked to how to improve Walmart's service. He told employees to visit the stores of competitors, not to steal their secrets, but to learn what they might do better at Walmart.

Walton was quoted as saying "Information is power, and the gain you get from empowering your associates more than offsets the risk of informing your competitors." (Walmart Inc., 2021). All these things enabled 'organizational intelligence' in Walmart to grow.

In general, for an organization to grow its organizational intelligence, members need to feel that they are treated fairly, and it also helps if the organization stands for a noble vision. Sam Walton's noble vision was "reducing the cost of living for everyone" (Walmart, 2014). And employees knew he meant it by his behavior. He usually drove an old pickup truck even when he became the world's richest man briefly before he died on April 5, 1992. Sam was constantly inventing pearls of wisdom which he would post in the stores. For example:

> There is only one boss. The customer. And he can fire everybody in the company from the chairman down, simply by spending his money somewhere else… Each Walmart store should reflect the values of its customers and support the vision they hold for their community…
>
> Outstanding leaders go out of their way to boost the self-esteem of their personnel. If people believe in themselves, it's amazing what they can accomplish…
>
> Nothing else can quite substitute for a few well-chosen, well-timed, sincere words of praise. They're absolutely free and worth a fortune (Walmart Inc., 2021)

The secret of success is not in these sorts of sayings *per se*, it's in the general noble spirit conveyed, along with the sense of caring, inspiring, and sharing with his associates.

Remarkably, these practices inspired hundreds of thousands of employees (associates) to feel that they were part of a team delivering real service at everyday low prices. Tactically, Sam was committed to cutting out the middleman and automating the supply chain whenever possible. In their relentless drive to reduce costs, Walmart became a leader in automation.

Automation, more than low salaries for employees, allowed Walmart to deliver goods at lower prices than any competitors. Walmart's learning network extended beyond employees. Walmart treated suppliers in much the same way as it treated employees, with respect and trust: the company opened their books to their suppliers, showing the costs for shelf space, and they also provided real-time access to company inventory and sales records with their Retail Link software.

Furthermore, to symbolically emphasize frugality and low cost, the company insists that it's senior executives stay two people in a hotel room when they are traveling to save money. This demonstrates to rank-and-file employees that everyone, including executives, must practice frugality.

In summary, the culture at Walmart reveals a set of pillars for organizational intelligence:

1. make everyone feel appreciated,
2. make everyone a part of a team,
3. treat everyone fairly (minimize hierarchy),
4. treat your suppliers as partners,
5. learn from outside information (customers) as well as inside information (associates),
6. have an inspiring vision,
7. cut out the middleman
8. automate when possible.

This last item, more than any other, is responsible for Walmart's dominance over the competition.

Automation is being driven by global increases in "intelligence" in all industries, a topic we will dive into in depth in chapter 10.

7.3 IDEO: Design Thinking and the Power of Empathy

IDEO was founded in 1991, by merging the design firm David Kelly Design with two other design firms owned by individuals Bill Moggridge and Mike Nuttall. It has subsequently become the most celebrated design firm in the world. IDEO is considered to be a leader not only in design, but in design thinking, a term they more or less coined and popularized. They offer courses in design thinking as well as offering management consulting and organizational design.

If you ask David Kelly or Tim Brown (CEO until 2019) what the key is to their success, and the success of design thinking as a whole, they will certainly mention empathy. By empathy, they mean being able to fully imagine and appreciate the point of view of customers. So, the trick to being a good designer is to always put yourself in the customer's shoes. However, empathy is only meaningful when surrounded by the other elements of their culture code/genes, which include a flat hierarchy (actually no hierarchy), equality, diversity, psychological safety for team members, and prototyping. By prototyping, I mean literally the trial-and-error testing of product ideas. You build it, test it, modify it, test it again, and so on until you converge on the final product. We just discussed the benefits of doing this. However, they also have other tools involving team meetings and sketching, drawing, and modeling tools, which all help them achieve their remarkable success.

Tim Brown has apparently conceived and put into practice at IDEO another behavior, in addition to the above set, which may be the single most important culture code/gene. The idea is expressed in this phrase: 'Your most important job is to help your colleagues succeed.' I don't know that Tim Brown actually said this, but it is certainly consistent with the spirit of his management philosophy.

According to a 2014 article in the Harvard Business Review by Teresa Amabile, Colin M. Fisher, and Julianna Pillemer, Tim Brown said "I believe that the more complex the problem, the more help you need. And that's the kind of stuff we're getting asked to tackle, so we need to figure out how to have a culture where help is much, much more embedded" (2014, 4).

The authors of the HBR report describe their studies of the activities, at a 47-person IDEO office, over a period of two years.

They built up a node diagram showing the connections of all employees who conversed with one another, with an indication of how much helping was going on shown by the size of the node. Upon viewing the node diagram, the first thing that leaps out at you is that everybody talked to everybody else. This is very unusual for most companies. The second thing that leaps out is the extensive amount of helping those employees gave each other.

A booklet was produced by IDEO (or people who work there) entitled The Little Book of IDEO (2016). It catalogs the key ideas in their culture code/ genes: it starts out "We wrote this to give you a sense of IDEO's culture—the ties that bind us together as coworkers and as people. These are the values that get us there." This very sentence reveals one of the most important genes in any organization. That gene is a sense of community. The people at IDEO like each other. The presentation continues with "be optimistic," "collaborate," "embrace ambiguity," "learn from failure" (ask for forgiveness, not permission), "make others successful," "take ownership," and "talk less, do more." (Nothing is worse than over-intellectualizing. Design is about rolling up your sleeves and making things.)

To connect the dots (as Steve Jobs used to say), let me comment these points.

Be optimistic: it's been proven that optimistic people recognize opportunities better than pessimists. In a talk delivered at Stanford University Technology Ventures Program in 2010, entitled "Core Values of Culture", Tony Hsieh, CEO and founder of Zappos, said they ask candidates for employment 'Do you consider yourself lucky?' They had discovered that 'lucky' people picked up more hidden clues in a test experiment in which two groups of people are given newspapers with hidden messages. They are told to count certain images, the headlines and text on the pages. But the newspapers have hidden messages telling them they are done and to mention a particular message to collect an extra $100. People who answered that they were lucky were much more likely to find the clue. People who earlier said they were not lucky failed to find the message at all.

Collaborate: what we must always bear in mind is that teams can be smarter than individuals. Collaboration means teaming, and teaming will usually produce superior results compared to people working alone.

Learn from failure: don't waste your time planning when you should be tinkering with "trial and error" real-world feedback.

Make others successful: this is the holy grail of collective intelligence. Going out of your way to help someone is the secret sauce of team building, as is accessing the group intelligence that can emerge from teams.

Talk less, do more: this is another way of saying build prototypes and benefit from real-world feedback, rather than spend time theorizing and planning.

IDEO has discovered a number of the genes that encode good behaviors that can increase organizational intelligence. They speak for themselves.

7.4 Google Alphabet: Indexing and Accessing the World's Information

Google is probably the most remarkable business on the planet for its contribution to humanity. It is also remarkable for its internal studies intended to enhance creativity and productivity. We will shortly look at its remarkable company culture, but first I'd like to acknowledge the technical genius of founders Sergei Brin and Larry Page.

First of all, the Google search engine gets smarter all the time, constantly learning from those who use it; a claim no other search engine can make. It gets smarter because of the nature of the PageRank algorithm. The PageRank algorithm says that the 'rank' of a 'page' (website) is proportional to the number of pointers to the page where each pointer is multiplied by the rank of the website originating the pointer. If you think about this for a moment, you realize that the rank of websites changes all the time. So, the system is always adjusting and constantly becoming more accurate because of the 'wisdom of crowds' voting scheme that is implicit in the PageRank algorithm. It is generally believed that the more people involved in rendering an opinion, the more accurate the opinion will be. This wisdom is built into the PageRank system by virtue of the 'voting' accomplished by the number of websites pointing to the website being ranked.

But there is more genius in the way they implemented their system. Before, Google internet web searches were made based on a library categorization system. It follows that every term in a search query belongs to a category and that the results returned are based on a summation of categories. Google came along and said we don't care about categories at all. We will simply find all the documents that contain the word you're looking for, ranked in a way that makes the most likely document percolate to the top. To do this required building an inverted index, which no one else had thought of doing and requires some programming genius to accomplish. And it took some genius to figure out it was practical to attempt it in the first place.[6]

And the technology story continues as they add other layers of phrase recognition to make it appear that Google actually understands natural language (e.g., English). Being able to converse in natural language with

[6]An inverted index means that Google is able to take any word and then tell you all the internet documents that contain that word rather than search for words within a document. Ever wonder why you can type any word in the Google search bar and be told that eight billion documents were searched for that word in 0.5 seconds? Of course, it's precomputed, but it took genius to figure out how to do it.)

a machine that can access all of human knowledge is the holy grail of AI research and will probably be the greatest gift to humanity that technology has ever produced.

So, it's important to acknowledge what Google is accomplishing before we move into their amazing company culture. Google has several extraordinary genes for growing organizational intelligence, including a truly noble vision, taking extraordinary care of its employees; an exceptionally good method for informing and soliciting opinions from employees. Google has been voted the best place to work in the USA year after year. They receive about two million applications a year for employment. Some of the attractions are good salaries, stock options, and seemingly the most extraordinary perks of any company on the planet. How can they afford to do it? It's part of the company culture and the fact that they are perfectly positioned to take advantage of the explosive growth of AI and internet social media. The company was founded in 1997 and in 13 short years grew to be among the world's most valuable companies, a position they still occupy today.

Part of Google's intelligence comes from self-reflection. It constantly studies its own internal operations. Google has probably studied its own team creativity and productivity more than any other company on the planet. Google is organized internally to be as flat as possible, minimizing inferred power differentials between managers and employees. Most of the powers of managers have been stripped away and replaced with peer review. And the effect of internal departments is minimized as employees are allowed to join different teams as an ever-expanding collection of networks of programmers. All the code is open source: everybody can see the computer code that goes into products.[7] But what's important is that information is shared and not hidden.

In 2012, Google hired a specialist to exclusively study teams and determine why some excelled and others stumbled. The study was called Project Aristotle, and it measured hundreds of teams for a couple of years. There is a good article describing the study entitled "What Google Learned from Its Quest to Build the Perfect Team" (2016).

The report's main conclusion was that psychological safety on teams mattered more than any other single thing they could measure. Psychological safety? What is that? Psychological safety means that people feel safe to speak up and say whatever is on their mind without worries about looking stupid or having a conflict with the boss. Google had just learned of Anita Woolley's

[7]As AI becomes more extensively used, "coding" is morphing into "training," using machine-learning and lots of data.

(2013) findings that equal turn-taking in collectively intelligent groups was critically important. Indeed, when group members felt psychological safety, they spoke more easily, and group participation balanced out.

However, there is more to the story. The most authoritative and complete description of ongoing studies since 2014 is to be found in the book titled *Work Rules* by Laszlo Bock, formerly Senior VP of People Operations at Google. Laszlo Bock gave an interview to CBS This Morning (2015a); he described the most important aspects of Google's culture, which are certainly different from traditional company cultures. He said the important points were:

1. An inspiring mission. How do we make the world a better place? In Google's case, 'organize the world's information and make it universally accessible and useful'
2. Information transparency. Board meeting minutes are shared with the rank-and-file employees.
3. Employee voice. Let everyone have a mechanism to influence important company decisions.
4. Removing power from managers. Managers cannot decide unilaterally whom to hire or fire, how someone's performance is rated, and whom to promote. These are all done by peer review.
5. Making jobs meaningful. This is done by connecting them to the overall mission of the company and others' well-being.
6. Trusting employees. Don't make them justify their decisions and give them the power to act without bureaucratic signoffs. Regularly ask them how they would change things to make them better (2015).

These are a few of the things that make Google one of the most intelligent companies on the planet.

7.5 Zappos: Delivering Happiness

The story of Zappos illustrates the extraordinary power of culture, as well as happiness on the job.

Zappos had (and perhaps still has) the most remarkable corporate culture of any company on the planet. It was the spiritual and financial creation of Tony Hsieh, a Chinese American born to Taiwanese parents. Zappos actually came into existence as ShoeSite.com; founded in 1999 by Nick

Swinmurn. It was on the verge of collapsing when Tony Hsieh, its angel financial backer and co-CEO, came on board full-time after the first year.

Its business model was to sell shoes online; all such businesses were collapsing in the year 2000. But Tony had a vision for the company which would see it deliver a personal emotional connection along with shoes it sold to customers. Tony renamed the company Zappos, invested more money, and set about creating a company culture consistent with delivering satisfaction, not simply a physical product. But this is getting ahead of the story. Let's back up to 1995.

After graduating from Harvard in 1995, Tony worked briefly for Oracle and then founded LinkExchange in his spare time. LinkExchange grew to 100 people and was acquired by Microsoft in 1998 for $265 million. Tony took his portion of the Microsoft money and became an angel investor, investing in ShoeSite.com as well as a few other companies. However, Tony had a life-changing epiphany while still working with LinkExchange employees. The epiphany was that the company culture mattered enormously to him, probably more than the money. He promised himself that, if he were to start another company, he would only hire people that he liked and would enjoy working with. And his goal was to deliver a spirit of happiness to employees and customers. So that's what he set about doing at Zappos.

And that's a major reason Zappos was able to grow to $1 billion sales by 2008. In 2009 Zappos had a revenue of $1.1 billion and was acquired by Amazon for roughly $940 million in Amazon stock and cash. It was the company culture that enabled this extraordinary success. It enabled Zappos to succeed when all the other dotcoms failed. And it not only succeeded, but it was also remarkably successful, more successful than any other company in its industry except maybe Amazon.

For the visitors and the press when they visit Zappos in Las Vegas, Nevada, the thing that stands out is the playground-like atmosphere in Zappos facilities. The other thing that is even more striking is the fact that all the employees seem to like each other; they are definitely effusive and playful in their verbal exchanges with each other. Tony had pulled off his vision. He had created a company with employees who believed in the company vision (offering delightful help to customers on the phone), had a sense of community, psychological safety, rich interpersonal communication networks, lots of encouragement to help each other, and the trust of the management. - This is an example of the lessons learned earlier, in Chapter 2, that contribute to collective intelligence.)

But the story doesn't stop there. Tony wrote a book called *Delivering Happiness* (2010). He wanted to understand the psychology behind employee happiness and share what he discovered. So, Tony shared that he subscribes to four principles that lead to employee happiness: 1. Give employees more perceived control, 2. Give employees opportunities to make progress, 3. Help employees feel connected, and 4. Provide a worthy vision / meaning.

In other words, to have happy employees (and therefore productive employees)

1. Involve employees in goal setting (perceived control)
2. Review performance frequently [formally at least twice a year] (perceived progress)
3. Organize individuals into teams (perceived connectedness)
4. Have a vision that inspires people and helps them find meaning (vision / meaning)

Furthermore, a great TED Talk by Shawn Achor, "The happy secret to better work," (2011) is all about the increase in productivity when employees are happy.

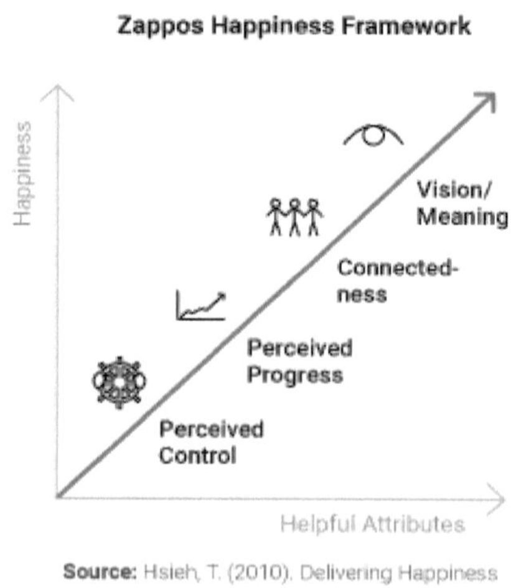

Figure 12: *Zappos Happiness Framework from Delivering Happiness*

Source: **Hsieh, 2010**

Another footnote to the genes of Zappos: Tony Hsieh has said that research shows that optimistic people tend to take more initiative and make better employees. So, he has job candidates read a newspaper and count the number of occurrences of certain words. But in the middle of the newspaper an 'Easter egg' is buried; a sentence that says in concept, 'You can stop reading now, and go to the end of the paper and collect a special reward for being alert'. Apparently optimistic people read this and follow the instructions, and pessimistic people slog on with their assigned task.

Tony conjectured that the rate of innovation in Zappos (and presumably other companies) was directly proportional to the number of ideas exchanged in conversations, especially casual conversations. He explicitly talks about (and tries to measure) the 'collision of ideas'. He reportedly said to a journalist, "I probably say the word *collision* a thousand times a day" (2018, 67). He attempts to arrange for the layout of buildings and rooms to cause people to bump into each other accidentally in an environment conducive to striking up conversations. The concept of collision of ideas is profound because the word *collision* indicates that it's not planned. In other words, nobody knows ahead of time who has good ideas, and what ideas are important, and where good ideas come from. However, it's often the case that when you bump into a good idea you can recognize it and add it to your mental collection.

Tony is the perfect leader of an innovative organization benefiting from 'the collision of ideas' because he doesn't suggest the ideas or impose his own ideas. He sets the stage for others to be creative, as stated by Linda Hill (2014). The best way to kill collective intelligence is for leaders to impose their own preconceived ideas on a group. The best way to promote collective intelligence is to hear from everybody and to give everybody equal footing[8].

More endorsement for the collision of ideas comes from Alex Pentland (2014) whose work we described in Chapter 2 & 3. Pentland showed that the more that people interacted with other people outside their immediate social circles, the more creative and innovative the people were. This is an amazing statement for its generality. The collision of ideas principle was also stated with different words by one of the principals of Y Combinator. He said in a documentary interview that the secret of Silicon Valley success was the density of highly qualified people that were likely to have chance encounters with others that could help start a business. He claimed that Sean Parker had bumped into Mark Zuckerberg in such fashion. And the results are legendary: Sean was able to convince Mark to leave Harvard and start a business in Silicon Valley which we know today as Facebook.

But the collision of ideas is just one more footnote to all the innovations that Tony Hsieh introduced to Zappos that promote organizational intelligence.

---

[8]Recall that to maximize the collective intelligence of a group, Anita Woolley proved that everyone must have equal floor time.

7.6 Zain: Corporate Intrapreneurship Done Right

Another noteworthy success that demonstrates how to inject entrepreneurial thinking into a company is Zain, a mobile phone company which started in the Middle Eastern country of Kuwait.

Zain was a state-owned phone company founded in 1983, originally called MTC (Mobile Telecommunications Company), with an annual revenue of roughly $250 million in 2002. Dr. Al Barrak joined them in 2002 as CEO when Zain became a private company. During the next six years, Zain expanded into 23 countries, and gross profit went from $250 million to $3.2 billion. It grew from having 0.5 million customers in 2002 to 75 million customers by 2009, while its market valuation went from $2.5 billion to more than $34 billion by 2007. By any measure, Zain was a phenomenal success.

Dr. Al Barrak accomplished this by instilling the entrepreneurial zeal appropriate for rapid expansion through giving high-level cultural guidelines for the company, not detailed orders. His organizational genes were the five F's, which he described in one a keynote address in 2015, as follows:

1. Future: Employees should be thinking about the future, about things they want to happen. Employees should imagine what they want and try to make their hopes come true. But plans need to be flexible and treated more as contingency planning; easy to change with healthy amounts of feedback from real-world testing.
2. Freedom: Freedom of expression is encouraged at all times, especially in meetings. Seniority should not matter. Everyone must be encouraged to speak at meetings, regardless of salary or position. Employees should also be free to work in any area they want. If you don't like your boss, you should be free to move to a different department.
3. Fortune: Employees should know that their financial well-being is a top priority, and that the company will try to increase their fortune as much as the fortunes of outside shareholders. To achieve this, stock options are essential for employees.
4. Fitness: In this case, fitness refers to social and technical fit with the company, 'We place 80% of our recruitment judgment on the character and values of the candidate. Only 20% weight is placed on technical skills'.

5. Fun: We recruit people that are optimistic and full of laughter because we want our work environment to be fun. When you're happy, you're working at your smartest capacity. You should not compete with others, but only with yourself, and have fun while you're doing it (2015).

Leadership, Dr. Al Barrak says, should be focused on creating a culture that delivers the five F's. It can be accomplished by a group as much as by a CEO. In fact, the top position should never be a one-man show. And the office of the CEO should be constantly promoting three things: ideas, relationships, and adventure.

Ideas: are the basis for corporate change, intellectual property development, and innovation. To get new ideas, employees should be encouraged to explore. But encouragement is not enough. You need harmonious relationships and a spirit of adventure.

Relationships: are to be continually promoted and strengthened by the CEO's office. The CEO's office needs to exude goodwill and promote relationships where everyone works in harmony and openness, and everyone feels included, competent, and significant.

Adventure: means a willingness to take risks, a bias toward action, with curiosity and courage. If employees know management is encouraging this, they will be more likely to take risks and initiative.

7.7 VISA International: Minimizing Hierarchy and the Chaordic Age

When the best leader's work is done, the people will say "we did it ourselves" Lao Tsu ~ 500 BC.

This summarizes the leadership model implemented at Visa International which grew from practically nothing at its founding in 1970 to become the world's largest financial organizations by the year 2000 with market capitalization in 2021 of more than $400 billion. It achieved this spectacular growth, at least partially, because of its innovative platform for organizational intelligence. The motive force for Visa was insight of one man, Dee Hock, who describes the journey of creating Visa in his book entitled *One from Many, Visa and the Rise of The Chaordic Organization* (2005).

Peter Senge, who wrote the excellent books *The Fifth-Discipline* (1990) and *The Dance of Change* (1999), wrote a foreword for Dee Hock's book which I highly recommend. Senge says it's amazing that the world's largest business, serving 1/6 of the world's population, is relatively invisible in the press. So, it is not widely understood and admired for what is. In fact, it invented and implemented a novel system of governance that pushes power away from a central focal point and distributes it broadly. It is unquestionably an improvement over most corporate structures, but few companies have tried it.

Visa International's CEO does not have an annual compensation nearly as high as CEOs of smaller companies, nor does Visa's CEO wield unilateral decision-making power given to CEOs of smaller companies. Yet Visa International is continually innovating and growing. It's member banks have the freedom to make changes without 'asking for permission' from a centralized authority. Visa is organized as a network, a federation, without reliance on a central authority deciding issues. It is run more as a capitalist democracy than a business. And that is its genius.

The organizational theory behind this was conceived by Dee Hock. He insisted that the Bank of America, which originally owned the dominant credit card franchise, should *not* have more control than any other member bank, if it were going to be possible to get competing banks to join the formation of a single credit card authority. This was a remarkable triumph because Bank of America could have dominated other credit card suppliers. But Dee Hock managed to convince the Bank of America of the merits of his theory of distributed control and Visa was born. Instead of a centralized management system, control was to be equally distributed to all the banks that participated. They should all have equal say. Hock decentralized management authority and distributed it broadly, giving member banks the authority to maximize their local profits as long as they abided by high-level rules of not jeopardizing other members.

Dee Hock's philosophy was captured in his widely known homily:

> "Heaven is purpose, principle, and people. Purgatory is paper and procedure. Hell is rules and regulations" (2005, 115).

In other words, he recommended giving people high-level guidelines (purpose and principle) and letting them make as many decisions as possible by themselves, unhampered by rules and regulations. This increases the number of minds involved in decision-making and thereby enhances the collective intelligence in the organization.

Dee Hock was inducted into the prestigious National Business Hall of Fame in 1991. He went on to write a book about his theory of management called *The Birth of the Chaordic Age* (1999), republished as the book *One from Many* (2005) in which he optimistically recommended that companies of the future minimize centralized control and operate as close as possible to the boundary of chaos as possible. Chaordic management would be the antithesis of hierarchical management, and its success speaks for itself.

Theodore Roosevelt insightfully said, "The best executive is the one who has sense enough to pick good men to do what he wants done, and self-restraint to keep from meddling with them while they do it (circa 1900). Following this advice increases collective intelligence by involving more people in decision-making.

7.8 Summary

Walmart, IDEO, Semco, Google, Zappos, Visa and Zain all differ from their respective competitors by the degree to which they broadly distribute information and power to act on it to more people in their companies. This promotes organizational intelligence by involving more people in decision-making. It is no coincidence that they are the most successful firms in their respective categories.

Organizations with greater intelligence always outperform competitors.

CHAPTER 8: STIMULATING ORGANIZATIONAL INTELLIGENCE

Promoting information discovery and transfer resulted from the various corporate cultures just described. In addition to what was described in Chapter 7, organizational intelligence can be promoted by financial rewards, workplace happiness, civility, and inspiring visions, all of which are now examined.

8.1 Financial Rewards

Does paying people more increase their productivity, creativity, or contribution to overall organizational intelligence?

Dan Pink wouldn't think so. In his delightful TED Talk, "The puzzle of motivation," delivered at TEDGlobal 2009, he reported on numerous experiments that demonstrate that problem-solving ability decreases the more participants are paid, at least in real-time problem-solving challenges.

It's fairly well documented that CEO compensation is not correlated with performance. In other words, paying CEOs higher salaries does not result in proportionally higher corporate performance. (This irony should embarrass the boards of directors of publicly traded companies for authorizing multimillion-dollar compensation packages for their CEOs. I hope for the good of the country that they come to their senses and stop this poisonous practice.) And what about the rank-and-file employees? Does paying them more result in higher performance? Holding out the prospect of higher pay for increased performance might result in higher productivity if you are poorly paid to start with, but it probably would not result in higher productivity once the compensation exceeds the threshold necessary for an employee to enjoy a lifestyle equivalent to their middle-class neighbors. What about paying individuals large bonuses to reward high performers? Attempting to preferentially reward individuals for performance that actually depends on a team is often counterproductive, because it can reduce team spirit, which would diminish collective intelligence. In any case, pay for performance based on a contribution to the bottom line is incredibly difficult to objectively implement. Consider the following.

Ronald Coase got a Nobel Prize in economics in 1991 for his paper "The Nature of the Firm," published in 1937, in which he said the transaction costs of paying employees as contractors would end up with employees receiving lower income than they would if they were on salary. In other words, attempting to share the income of a firm with the members of the firm based on some sort of merit-based revenue-sharing model is impractical because of the amount of overheads that the employer must spend to compute individual contributions. And this is why firms exist with salaried employees rather than bonus-compensated employees. Anytime a company rewards its members separately and individually, as is usually the case, it tends to reduce proactive information-sharing because members know their salary/bonus is based on their individual performance rather than team performance. It is better to explicitly reward an entire team. However, blending individual and team compensation is reasonable as long as the team component is substantial.

The goal of any reward system must be to increase communication between people in the firm. There are many ways of accomplishing this, including free group lunches and enjoyable common areas. A great way of promoting communication is to provide a stimulating environment such as offered by Google, with toys and novel constructions throughout their premises. This promotes communication and the collision of ideas that occurs when people linger publicly instead of staying in their offices. One way of helping people appreciate each other is to pay attention to workplace civility and incivility as described by Christine Porath (2018).

8.2 Workplace Civility

In an ideal working environment, the CEO and direct reports and staff would radiate optimism, lack of stress, and courteous behavior. As we shall see, this sort of behavior spreads like a virus and increases both the creativity and the mental abilities of people. It also motivates them to share information. In contrast, incivility at the top can also radiate through an organization. Incivility is subtle, but it basically means being impolite, and using negative terminology or negative body language to communicate publicly or privately.

In a wonderful TED Talk given by Christine Porath, TED, University of Nevada, in 2018, entitled "Why being respectful to your coworkers is good for business," Christine starts out by explaining that incivility can be bad for a person's health and may also damage corporate success.

She said, "We sent a survey to business school alumni working in all different organizations. . . what we found is that incivility as just defined made people less motivated: 66 percent cut back work efforts, 80 percent lost time worrying about what happened, and 12 percent left their job." Having people leave their jobs or be sulky on the job hurts the bottom line in many corporations. Upon hearing about Christine's work, she says that Cisco reported that they estimated conservatively that they lost $12 million a year due to uncivil behavior.

Incivility takes on many forms and it can include simply ignoring someone, or more aggressive comments such as: 'That's stupid,' 'That's not how it's done,' or 'If I wanted your opinion, I'd ask.'

One of the most important aspects of incivility is that it affects us subconsciously and spreads in organizations from person to person, like a virus. People tend to treat other people as they have been treated.

Porath (2018) says that little things such as how you say good morning in the hallway, with eye contact and a smile, or listening attentively, can end up making people feel respected, heard, and appreciated. On the other hand, a lack of genuine contact can make them feel small, insulted, disregarded, or excluded. But there's more to it. People can be affected by simply observing how other people are being treated rather than experiencing impolite treatment themselves. And they can be affected simply by seeing rude words in any context. Consider Porath's next experiment. She recounts an experiment in which they gave people combinations of 15 words to make up a sentence. She said (approximately): Half the participants got a list with 15 words used to trigger rudeness: words like impolitely, interrupt, obnoxious, bother. The other half received a list of words with none of the rude triggers. People who got the rude words were five times more likely to miss information right in front of them on the computer screen. Furthermore, those that read the rude words took longer to make decisions, to record their decisions, and they made significantly more errors.

She then told the story of an uncivil doctor who yelled at a medical team. Shortly thereafter the team administered drugs to a patient, but they gave the wrong amounts. Even though the correct information was right there on the chart, somehow everyone on the team missed it. In this case, the patient died. People exposed to rudeness didn't share information as readily, nor seek help from their teammates. This is poisonous to collective intelligence. It has been documented that medical teams exposed to incivility perform worse in diagnosis and performing procedures. Porath concludes by saying someone did an academic study at a Center for Creative Leadership and found that the number one reason tied to executive failure was an insensitive, abrasive, or bullying style. Abrasive leaders would find it practically impossible to exploit the collective intelligence in the organization around them. Success or failure in any company or team is determined by the degree to which collective intelligence is utilized.

It's clear that civility in the workplace promotes organizational intelligence and incivility kills it.

8.3 Workplace Happiness

Shawn Achor in his popular TED Talk "The happy secret to better work" (TEDxBloomington, 2011) describes the effect of happiness on job performance. He essentially said that happy employees are significantly more creative and productive than neutral or unhappy employees. Furthermore, optimism, an artifact of happiness, is significantly more important to job success than IQ. He went on to describe what he called the 'happiness advantage' of companies with happy employees.

He said "your brain at positive performs significantly better than at negative, neutral or stressed. Your intelligence rises, your creativity rises, your energy levels rise. In fact, we've found that every single business outcome improves. Your brain at positive is 31% more productive than your brain at negative, neutral or stressed. You're 37% better at sales. Doctors are 19 percent faster, more accurate at coming up with the correct diagnosis when positive instead of negative, neutral or stressed" (2011)

Reuters, in 2021, commented that when BlackRock, the world's largest asset manager, evaluates potential stock purchases, they consider employee sentiment. BlackRock said, "Happy and engaged employees lead to more wins and more sales opportunities" (Toonkel, 2015). They use data from social media websites, including employee sentiment data, such as comments from Glassdoor.

Glassdoor solicits input from company employees indicating how happy they are with their employer. So, their results are generally taken as an indication of happiness on the job.

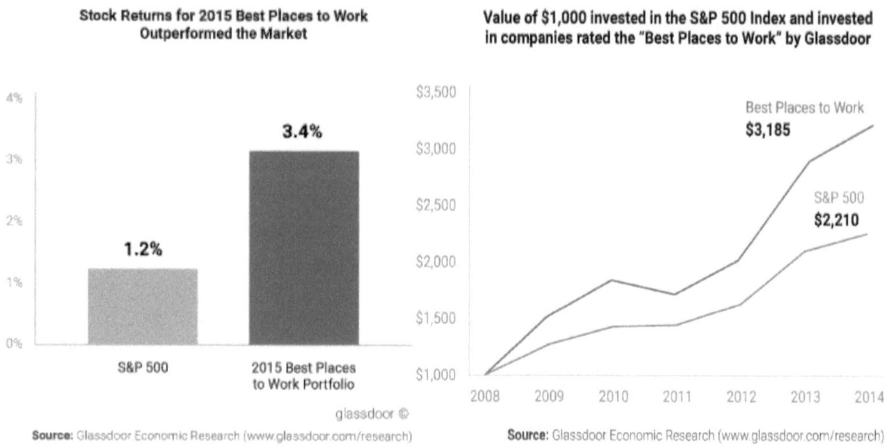

Figure 13: *Women affecting share price*

Source: ***Glassdoor (2014 - 2015)***.

The data confirms that having happy employees helps companies be more creative and productive, as reflected in their superior stock price performance. Employees will be happier when they feel they are appreciated, and / or they like the people they work with, and / or are working toward a larger vision that they find inspiring.

8.4 Workplace Vision: The Impact of Idealism

In industrialized nations where employees earn enough money to take care of their basic life needs (apparently about $80,000 annually in the USA), they can have the luxury of working for causes they believe in, 'to make the world a better place', rather than simply working for money. People like to think their time is benefiting others in addition to themselves.

Knowledge workers (most of us) are more motivated, creative, and inspired when their organization is committed to a larger vision: sustainability, social responsibility, or improving the quality of life of customers or the community in which they operate (see Figure 14).

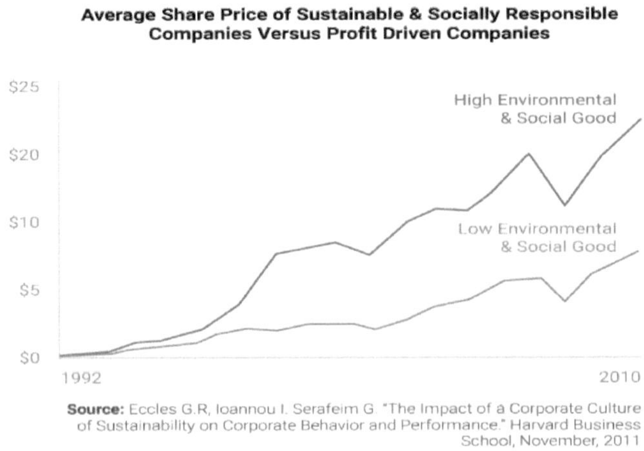

Figure 14: *Average Share Price of Sustainable & Socially Responsible Companies Versus Profit Driven Companies*

Source: ***Eccles, Ioannou, Serafeim, 2011***

People are actually more intelligent and creative when they believe their efforts are serving a higher purpose. And the share price of company stock reflects this. One of the most inspiring of all corporate vision statements is that of Google. Google's vision says, "Our company mission is to organize the world's information and make it universally accessible and useful." (Google, 2021). They are probably doing more than any other company on the planet to increase organizational intelligence in the countries they serve, by providing access to the world's information based on natural language queries. But the point is that this sort of noble vision inspires Google employees and helps them be more creative and intelligent in tackling their activities.

B Corp companies also undoubtedly get intelligence lift from the noble vision they hold. In order to join the informal Federation of B Corp companies, a company must ascribe to, and prove they are compliant with, the B Corp Declaration of Interdependence, which states

> That we must be the change we seek in the world.
>
> That all businesses ought to be conducted as if people and place mattered.
>
> That, through their products, practices, and profits, businesses should aspire to do no harm and benefit all.
>
> To do so requires that we act with the understanding that we are each dependent upon another and thus responsible for each other and future generations (B Lab, 2021). See also Appendix 3.

SECTION 3: NATIONAL ORGANIZATIONAL INTELLIGENCE

CHAPTER 9: NATIONAL BUSINESS ECOSYSTEMS

The same principles of intelligence that promote business success also promote the success of entire nations, and vice versa. So, there is much to be learned that applies to business by studying the evolution of nations. The customs, constitutions, and laws that national governments need to survive and prosper have been selected through evolution. We can forecast national economic outcomes by understanding this evolution as the evolution of intelligence at a national level.

9.1 The Evolution of Nations and Civilizations

In Chapter 3 we saw through the work of Alex Pentland (2014) how by analyzing mobile phone data the farther people traveled, and the more interactions they had with people as they traveled, the wealthier and more prosperous they were. This is a microcosm of what has been happening with humanity over thousands of years. When our forebears traveled several thousand years ago, they made discoveries, collected information, and formed alliances, tribes, and nations. They were definitely wealthier and more prosperous for having done so.

As a youth, I used to wonder why modern civilization evolved first in the northern hemisphere. And why did it happen in the Old World (Eurasia) as opposed to the New World (the Americas)? Why is it taking so long for Africa to catch up? Was there something important about having seasons as opposed to the more uniform climate of the tropics? Is civilization simply a matter of reaching a critical mass of people and which takes a long time to reach?

The answer to these questions probably comes from the collision of ideas granted to humanity by the geography of where they lived. The rate of population growth did not change much in 40,000 years until the transition from hunter gatherers to farming which occurred around 6,000 years ago. Then, the rate of population growth more or less exploded about 150 years ago; the rate of economic growth changed dramatically with the Industrial Revolution in Europe. Why did this giant leap forward start in Europe and not China, or the New World, or any other place on the globe?

Why did it take nearly 55,000 years, ever since evolution gave us our current form and we came 'out of Africa', for this giant leap forward to happen? Large populations were thriving for thousands of years in China and India, and somewhat in Europe, but nothing like what we see today. Plots of the estimated total number of humans on the planet were relatively flat for 55,000 years, and then took a steep turn upwards starting 150 years ago.

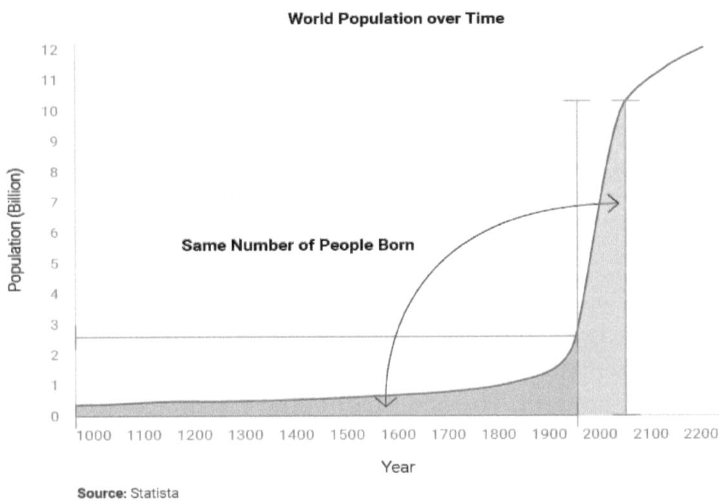

Figure 15: *World Population Over Time*

Source: ***Statista (2021)***

A couple of hundred years ago, something happened for the first time in 50,000 years with the invention of the machinery that created the Industrial Revolution. The knock-on effect of this machinery has been advances in medicine and science which eventually prolonged people's lives. The key question is 'Why were northern European countries the first to harness the power of water, steam and surface coal reserves in concert with the building of factories?'

Surprisingly, our pets and domesticated animals hold the secret to a profound insight. In the 15th century, Europeans discovered and invaded the New World. They discovered that the indigenous people had none of the European domesticated animals (such as horses, goats, sheep, chickens, pigs, camels, cats, and dogs). Most human diseases come from domesticated animals. So New World Indians had no immunities to the diseases Europeans brought with them. Scholars such as Pringle (2015) estimate that more than 99% of the deaths that followed the European conquest of the New World came from disease, not military action.

So why did Europeans have all these animals? And why did the New World inhabitants have none?

You can probably answer this question by looking at a map of the world. The answer has to do with the geography of the continents and travel by foot. The European and Asian continents are contiguous and largely sited in the temperate zone. People were able to literally walk almost one-quarter of the distance around the globe, and stay in the same temperate zone, on habitable landmass. And they did. They walked and traded, and also collected animals, pets, and domesticated herds and flocks. And most importantly, they also collected knowledge along the way. The collected knowledge eventually gave rise to tempered steel, cannons, guns, heavy weaponry, steam engines, sailing ships, and the Industrial Revolution.

And eventually, using this technology which they got by being a world center for international trade, the little island nation of Great Britain acquired a launchpad to conquer the world. But trade was only half the reason for GB's strength. The other half of the explanation comes from the country's government.

China was also a trading nation. China was vastly superior in terms of population and landmass. Why didn't China do better than Great Britain? The critical difference seems to lie with their systems of government.

9.2 The Rise of Great Britain

It has been said that in the world of commerce ideas are exchanged as well as goods, even if not for money.

Great Britain and China both traded goods, for sure, but were not equally able to take advantage of the ideas they exchanged. The Chinese did not 'learn' as quickly as the British. The reasons are profound and of great relevance for modern politics.

Starting 6,000 years ago empires were springing up in both China and the Middle East. And by 2,000 years ago two mighty empires flourished around Rome in the Mediterranean and Beijing in Chinese East Asia. The Roman Empire lasted about 400 years and boasted a population of about 50 million people. At the same time in China, the Han dynasty reigned, and it had a similar population to the Roman Empire. The Roman Empire (at least the western half that involved Rome) fell apart in AD 476 whereas the Chinese Han dynasty continued. Chinese craftsmen went on to invent silk, the compass, paper, tea, kites, gunpowder, the first printed book, movable type, and explosives all before AD 1500.

A striking example of the Chinese superiority to Europe in 1500 can be seen by comparing the size of ships at that time. In 1492, when Columbus discovered and conquered the New World, Columbus only had three ships. Each was roughly 85 feet and carried 50 men. Or perhaps a better example would be the apex of European naval strength, the Spanish Armada. It was the greatest collection of ships Europe had ever seen when, in 1588, Spain attempted to conquer England. They had 130 ships, each carrying about 700 soldiers.

By comparison and at the same time, the Chinese Emperor commissioned - not due to war, but for amusement - Zheng He to explore the oceans nearby. Zheng He commanded a fleet of 300 ships (more than double the Spanish Armada's 130), which each accommodated 2,000 passengers each (compared to 700 in the Spanish Armada). His larger ships stretched 400 feet in length (approximately 5 times the length of the Spanish ships) with nine-masted giant junks called bao chuan in Chinese meaning treasure ships The Chinese boats were transporting a valuable cargo of porcelains, silks, lacquerware, and fine-art objects, which would be exchanged for the treasures sought by the Middle Kingdom China such as ivory, rhinoceros' horn, tortoiseshell, rare woods and incense, medicines, pearls, and precious stones. This armada of Chinese ships carried up to 28,000 sailors and soldiers on four tiers of decks (Levathes, 1994).

Zheng He took his ships all around Southeast Asia, visiting such places as Ceylon, Thailand, islands in Indonesia, and as far as the Middle East. He brought back many trophies and animals. So, China in the 1500s was unquestionably stronger and more powerful than Spain or any country in Europe. But what happened next is astonishing and reveals the reason that China eventually lost out in the race to the Industrial Revolution.

After Zheng He died at Calicut on the Indian coast, the Chinese armada never sailed again. The emperors fortified the Great Wall and barricaded themselves inside. The Chinese Emperor had the fleet burned and all oceangoing expeditions were banned. The information and records brought back were destroyed. Building a ship with more than two masts became a capital offense in 1500. Even putting to sea in one was a crime fifty years later (Crowley, 2015).

This destruction of technical knowledge happened explicitly and implicitly many times during the dynastic years in China. Emperors would simply order books burned, or otherwise destroy anything that would give power to potential threats to the Throne.

But that's not the whole story. What happened in Europe was starkly different. In contrast to China, Europe had no central empire after Rome fell, most of Europe was transformed into a collection of competing nations, fiefdoms, and large tribes holding dominion over nearby geographical areas. The mountainous terrain made natural boundaries, so the region had many small kingdoms with no central emperor. There was little interference from a central government with trade and commerce, or technology development.

China had no such competition between states or provinces. It had no need to continuously refine its steel production, or cannons, or industrial machinery. And ironically, the emperors of China actually interfered with the accumulation of knowledge, by banning any developments that look like they might threaten the power of the throne. Thus, China did not accumulate the technology required for an Industrial Revolution.

By 1900 Great Britain was the richest in the world; it had the largest military, it was the center of world business and finance, it had the strongest educational system, and its currency was the world standard of value (Michie, 2017) . And it had the highest standard of living. In fact, the small island of Great Britain was able to dominate the huge nations of India and the Chinese dynastic empire in the 1800s, at a time when China probably had 300 million people, India had 150 million people, and Great Britain had 10 million people.

The fundamental reason Great Britain was able to leap ahead of China is that Great Britain was able to harness the power of democratic laissez-faire capitalism. In contrast China was ruled by emperors, with top-down management hierarchy. Little Great Britain emerged so powerful it could conquer China, India, and dominate much of the developing world by the 19th century . . . because of three advantages which can each be seen as providing the build blocks for Great Britain's success:

1st reason: Geography 1: Great Britain had coastlines that facilitated sailing ships and international trade and commerce to the Americas (from Liverpool), to the content (from London), and to the global Empire hence the exchange of innovative ideas being brought in from traveling around the world in pursuit of trade.

2nd reason: Geography 2: Europe had mountains that provided obstacles to centralized control, which meant Europe had no emperor, no dynasties, no central authority blocking competition between small kingdoms and fiefdoms.

3rd reason: Democracy: Great Britain on several occasions, starting with the Magna Carta in AD 1215, saw insurrections in which groups of lords and rulers of localized fiefdoms were able to gain concessions from the king, limiting the power of the king. Thus, the foundations for democracy were gradually laid. And even though Great Britain had a king or queen, it was already a fledgling representative democracy.

Democracy is critically important to the development of national economies because it provides infrastructure for business without the centralized control that thwarts the innovation, creativity, and initiative required for entrepreneurship.

9.3 The Curse of Centralized Planning

Over and over again during the 50 years I've been observing business successes and failures, I've seen countless examples of strong CEOs with grand visions for their companies who failed. Strong leadership typically results in centralized planning that revolves around the individual CEO's biases. It made me wonder if there was a causal relationship between centralized planning and business failure. Furthermore, could the same phenomenon be observed in nations as well as business organizations.

Consider the USA. It was founded on the belief there should be no king, but rather government should be based on democratic principles. In fact, the framers of the Constitution were absolutely adamant there should never be anything approximating a king. So, the Constitution divided the federal government into three branches (the Legislative Branch, the Executive Branch, and the Judicial Branch) to make sure no individual or group could gain too much power. The goal was to push power away from the federal government out to states and citizens in general.

It is exactly what is needed to promote the growth of national organizational intelligence. The USA is the powerhouse it is today because it minimizes government control and maximizes individual freedoms which thereby increases opportunities for the growth of organizational intelligence.

Other striking contrasts between democracy and central planning can be seen in North Korea versus South Korea, the USSR versus the USA, historic Great Britain versus China.

For most of the last 500 years, Great Britain was a relatively small democratic nation, in contrast to China and India, which between them possessed half the world's population. China was ruled by an emperor with absolute authority. India was a collection of small kingdoms with no significant national government. Great Britain was able to dominate these huge countries because democracies do such a better job of distributing information and allowing entrepreneurs to act on it.

Looking again at China in the 20th century, *Mao Zedong* was founder and Chairman of the People's Republic of China and leader of the Chinese Communist Party in defeating the Chinese Nationalist government in 1949. His proclamations were treated as mandates from heaven. In 1958, Mao Zedong asked Chinese farmers to donate their metal farm equipment to make factories in his Great Leap Forward policy between 1958 and 1962. This policy led to the starvation and deaths of up to 45 million people – easily making it the biggest episode of mass murder ever recorded. And this was all a result of centralized planning.

North Korea offers another example of the failure of centralized planning. There has been widespread starvation in North Korea for the past 25 years, in contrast to its sibling, South Korea which has abundant prosperity. There are a few places on earth that demonstrate the differences in economic outcomes between totalitarian rule and democracy so dramatically as North and South Korea. Prior to 1945, Korea was a single nation occupying the Korean Peninsula. Except for 35 years when it was conquered and occupied by the Japanese, it had remained a single nation for thousands of years until 1945. Then at the end of World War II, with Japan defeated, the country was divided into two zones: North and South of the 38th parallel. The Americans occupied and administered the southern zone, below the 38th parallel, called South Korea, while the USSR (Union of Soviet Socialist Republics) administered the northern half.

The USSR set up a typical Socialist state in North Korea which was essentially a dictatorship. The organizational genes set forth in the Constitution of North Korea gave dictatorial powers to the supreme leader with no pretext of democracy.

It's important to note that the organizational genes that the USSR bequeathed North Korea were not evolved, and that the USSR itself later decayed and fell apart. In other words, these were inferior genes.

In North Korea, economic activity was centrally planned, and citizens were not allowed to own property. On the other hand, in South Korea, the Americans instilled a democratic form of government with laissez-faire capitalism modeled after the American system of governance. The organizational genes here had undergone hundreds of years of evolution way back to the democratic beginnings of Great Britain. Private ownership of property was a fundamental pillar. Entrepreneurial activity was actively encouraged.

Initially the effects of governance were obscured by the Korean War, from 1950 to 1953. During the war North Korean soldiers overran 90% of South Korea, followed by South Korea being aided by UN forces running over 90% of North Korea. This incited mainland China to enter the war on the side of North Korea which nearly defeated American and South Korean forces. During this time American bombers practically obliterated all industry in North Korea. But an armistice was reached in 1953 and both sides rebuilt their economies. The ensuing years revealed the effects of democratic capitalism versus dictatorship. Year after year, the economic gap between the two economies widened. In satellite imagery taken at night, South Korea looks like a Christmas tree, flooded with light, evidence that South Korea has one of the most prosperous economies on earth. On the other hand, North Korea is completely black showing that North Korea has practically no economy at all.

The internet abounds with satellite images showing the stark visual contrast between North and South Korea. In addition to the lack of lights, we know from interviews with North Koreans who have escaped, there has been widespread starvation in North Korea for the last 30 years. In fact, in the late 1990s dead bodies were stacked up in the streets, starvation was so rampant. There is no other explanation for this economic disaster other than governmental genes. . . in the constitutions of these two nations. Korea had started as a single nation, and there is no reason why people living north of the 38th parallel should start starving while people living south had an abundance of everything. North Korea started out with the same ethnicity, same language, same access to resources, same work ethic, same level of education, and same technology. In South Korea, democracy and capitalism clearly increased the number of minds involved in knowledge acquisition and decision-making, and thereby allowed organizational intelligence to grow over time. The more intelligent an organization is, the better it can take care of its people. As Figure 16 graphically illustrates, the brightly lit area in the lower right is South Korea; and the brightly lit area in the upper left is mainland China. The black hole in the middle is North Korea.

Figure 16: *Satellite image of North and South Korea*

Source: ***Earth Science & Remote Sensing Unity, NASA Johnson Space Center (2014)***

Another example of the failure of centralized planning is the decay of the USSR which, 50 years ago, was the largest nation on earth with more natural resources than any other nation in the world. It was nominally a union of a dozen socialist republics, but in practice the government and the economy were centrally managed by the Communist Party in Moscow, Russia. Remarkably, it was exposure to outside information coming from satellite TV in the 1980s that caused the country to dissolve in 1991. Images poured into the USSR of life in Western European nations where life was visibly much more prosperous. All Soviet citizens could see that the centralized planning and government policies coming out of Moscow were inferior to Western democracies. So, the governments of the satellite nations withdrew from the union.

The rise and fall of empires and nations are usually failures of centralized planning. It is easy to identify the government practices that lead to the failures. However, there is a hidden corollary of government centralized planning in the commercial world: namely, income disparity and the rise of the super wealthy. It is the accretion of wealth and power by wealthy individuals and corporations around the world to the point that economic decision-making takes place by exceedingly wealthy individuals or companies, and this becomes de facto centralized planning.

A few years ago, I watched Hans Rosling show statistics that better health, wealth, and longevity were spreading to all nations on the planet (2009). It appeared that the gradual sharing of knowledge and technology was allowing all countries to conquer disease and have more productive lives. I naturally assumed that economic parity between nations would soon be reached. Then I was startled to see other statistics that show that the wealth gap between rich countries and poor countries is actually increasing! In other words, rich countries are getting wealthier more rapidly than poor countries were, despite information and technology sharing through better telecommunications links and international trade partnerships.

The primary answer as to why this is the case has to do with the exponential rate of industrial automation as Chapter 10 discusses. A secondary reason has to do with the economic damage done by wealth concentration in the hands of the super wealthy. This is discussed by heavyweight scholar Thomas Piketty in the next section.

9.4 Thomas Piketty: Insights into Capital and Ideology

One of the consequences of industrialization and laissez-faire capitalism is the migration of wealth into the hands of wealthy individuals. When this becomes extreme, it reduces the organizational intelligence of the countries.

In his books Capital and Ideology (2019), and Capital in the 21st Century, (2013) Thomas Piketty showed that the rate of return for invested capital has always been higher than the GDP growth rate of the economy in the many countries he checked. Furthermore, this was true in all Western European nations and the USA since they started keeping records, approximately 1,000 years ago. This means that wealthy individuals who invest in capital have always made more money than people who work for a living. In other words, the rich get richer faster than poor people do.

Historically, when the imbalance got too high, there were popular revolutions and governments were overthrown. For example, the French Revolution from 1789–1799, which killed tens of thousands of innocent people, was actually a rebellion against the rich. The wealth imbalance, and common knowledge of it facilitated by the printing press, provoked many imbalanced nations in Europe to have their own revolutions shortly thereafter (Gildea, 1987). However, these revolutions usually resulted in the loss of social law and order. With the possible exception of the United States, none of the revolutions resulted in an orderly transition to more democratic rule.

The parallels with contemporary events such as the Arab Spring of 2010 are striking. Piketty (2019) observed that income inequality was quite high in Europe before the First World War and probably contributed to the civil unrest that motivated the war. In other words, citizens' awareness of the unequal distribution of wealth was one of the indirect causes of the First World War (see topincomes.parisschoolofeconomics.eu). War or rebellion may not be the only outcome of inequality. It is profoundly interesting that the US and the world entered a global recession in 1929 when wealth inequality was at its peak. So, general economic malaise or depression can result from widespread wealth inequality as well.

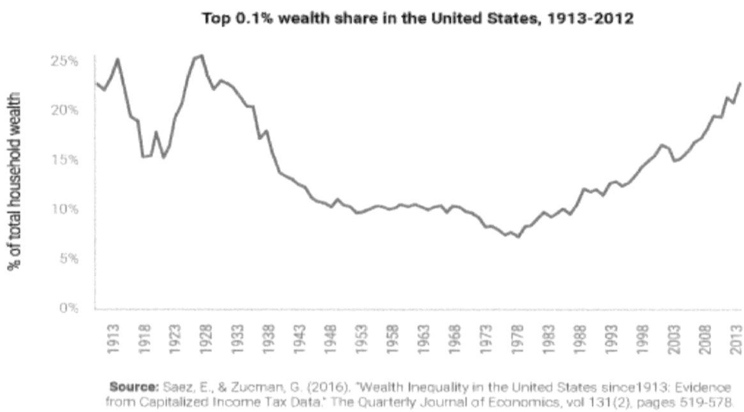

Figure 17: *Top 0.1% wealth share in the United States, 1913-2012*

Source: ***Saez and Zucman, 2016, pp. 519-578.***

From Figure 17 we can see that inequality was highest at the onset of the world's Great Depression in 1929. We can also see that we are now entering the zone of high inequality again. You would be justified in assuming a causal relationship between wealth distribution and economic progress. Or the flipside may be true: concentration of wealth may bring on recessions.

In 2016, the 62 richest people on the planet owned as much as the poorest 50% according to Oxfam, that is 3.7 billion people. But the problem is getting worse. The number declined from 86 to 26 as of 2019. Part of the problem is that the super wealthy make their money from international business, which enables tax havens. On the other hand, every rich person has to be a citizen of some country, and that country could take responsibility for taxation according to international standards. The machines and the infrastructure that make modern billionaires are what all of our ancestors worked on and contributed to, not simply the latest generation. There needs to be a mechanism for putting wealth generated by machines back in that society rather than giving it to single individuals. When wealth is more equitably distributed, countries prosper. In an interview with Bloomberg, February 2020, Piketty said "The enormous growth in prosperity that came in the 20th century through most of the world was achieved by a reduction in inequality" (Bloomberg Markets & Finance, 2019).

When we look at Figure 17 it is not unreasonable to wonder whether the enormous growth and prosperity in the US will continue much longer. And even though the USA ranks sixth in the world in terms of GDP per capita, this has not resulted in national happiness. Note that the US ranked number 14 in the *World Happiness Report* in 2021. To help mitigate the problem, Piketty suggests that nations should consider levying a wealth tax as well as a guaranteed minimum income to protect against the current trends toward wealth inequality. Note that organizational intelligence would be increased in a country where wealth is more equitably distributed.

9.5 Lessons from Highly Successful Countries

Only two of the top ten richest nations have more than five million people—Switzerland with seven million, and the USA with 331 million. Furthermore, there has been a global trend for larger nation-states to split, and as of 2003, half the world's countries had a population smaller than the average American state (about six million).

The Economist magazine of December 20, 2003 carried an article examining the prosperity of countries based on population size. The article observed that the wealthiest nations in terms of GDP per capita were also the smallest nations.

To further punctuate the advantages of being small, it should be noted that Switzerland is not a country in the usual sense, but a federation of cantons that have the right to self-govern on local issues. They each have local taxes and sometimes speak different languages. Switzerland has the highest nominal wealth per adult, the eighth-highest per capita GDP, and its large cities (such as Zürich, Geneva, and Basel) rank among the highest in the world in terms of their qualities of life. All this lends credibility to the argument that 'small is beautiful' and to the contention that government decision-making in smaller units may be more intelligent than that which occurs in larger nations.

Richest Countries in the World and their Population

Ranking	Country	GDP (USD per capita)	Population
1	Luxembourg	143,203	626 Thousand
2	Ireland	112,769	4.94 Million
3	Switzerland	96,788	8.65 Million
4	Norway	95,165	5.42 Million
5	Denmark	78,068	5.79 Million
6	United States	77,653	331 Million
7	Singapore	75,250	5.76 Million

Source: Wikipedia (2020)

Figure 18: *Richest Countries in the World and their Population*

Source: ***Wikipedia (2020)***

Looking at Figure 18, it seems that smaller countries manage their economies better on a per capita basis than the larger ones. This is possibly related to greater citizen involvement in smaller nations. It's no coincidence that people in smaller countries are also happier. In general, wealth, happiness, small size, and equality are correlated. The lessons we learned earlier about collective intelligence would actually predict this outcome, i.e., greater equality implies more equal access to information and greater freedom to act on it. For larger countries, a way of mitigating the effects of size is to have smaller governing subunits, such as provinces, municipalities, states, and cities that take responsibility for more of the things people care about, health, education, and welfare; with responsibility for only national defense and national infrastructure (roads, highways, telecommunications/ internet) being left in the hands of federal (or national) governments.

9.6 The Genes of Singapore

Singapore was described in Chapter 1. This is an elaboration upon the genes of the Singapore economy.

1. Lee Kuan Yew made it abundantly clear that the government was to be a true unflinching meritocracy. Government appointments and contracts were to be transparent and based on merit, not wealth or lobbyists.

2. He advocated that the government should create media campaigns to promote law-abiding, moral behavior.
3. Religious freedom was not simply guaranteed but celebrated: Christian, Hindu, and Muslim holidays were observed as national holidays.
4. Corruption and bribery were effectively abolished by very publicly jailing ministers who accepted any sort of special favors from businessmen. Singapore is considered the least corrupt country in Asia.
5. A world-class educational system was instituted to provide a highly trained workforce and talented government functionaries.
6. To attract the best and the brightest into government positions, relatively high salaries were offered.
7. Important decisions impacting the economy were to be based on advice from outside scholars and experts. They regularly invited world experts to fly to Singapore to advise government ministers.
8. To encourage business, they offered low tariffs and minimal government red tape.
9. They set up and heavily funded a highly successful Economic Development Board. The EDB offered subsidies to attract multinationals to set up manufacturing plants in Singapore.
10. The EDB also focused on and emphasized banking and shipping. It's worth noting that Singapore now has the busiest seaport in the world and is a bustling financial center.
11. They allowed private ownership of real estate and commercial assets.

Over the years, Singapore has been masterful at learning the needs of its economy and inventing solutions as needed. Singapore invented dozens of statutory boards, each with their own mandate and budget. Examples include, amongst others, the EDB (Economic Development Board), the HDB (Housing Development Board), the Land Transport Authority, and the National Parks Board. The titles are self-explanatory, and their successes remarkable; for example, more than 80% of Singaporeans live in housing provided by HDB (Government of Singapore, 2021).

Singapore has also sponsored many dozens of 'Government Linked Corporations', in which the government holds significant share ownership. By the mid-1980s Singapore owned 87 such GLCs and over the years has invested in more than 400 companies. Its sovereign wealth fund, composed primarily of these investments, is worth more than $1 trillion which puts its value among the top half dozen sovereign funds in the world.

Singapore's evolved parliamentary democracy has velvet glove censorship and has the benefit of being able to make decisions without the public polarization created by media in US and British democracies. This results in improved collective intelligence because legislators are better able to engage in deliberative discussions rather than pandering to the media. Collective intelligence in government also benefits from the fact that legislators are better educated and paid more than in Western democracies.

In short, Singapore's intelligence grew with time, guided by the organizational genes (morals, biases, laws, and philosophy) motivated by Lee Kuan Yew. It brings in technology, industry, and ideas from the outside world and provides a social safety net for citizens. There are many aspects to running a successful economy, more than we can hope to put down in writing here. But it is of paramount importance to continually solicit new information from the outside world and continually adapt internally.

9.7 Why Nations Fail

Nations fail for the same reasons that businesses fail; lack of intelligent planning, and failure to build the infrastructure needed for success. Sometimes they fail for lack of national defense. But there are more subtle reasons as well. We will not, in this short section, begin to answer this question adequately. However, we will be able to show how genes for national success get passed down through cultural biases when nations are being formed.

James Robinson in his 2012 book *Why Nations Fail,* stated that the governments that succeed have constitutions that keep power in the hands of the people, and prevent power migrating into the hands of an oligarchy. This is a wonderful statement because it is yet another way of saying that the intelligence of an organization increases when more people are engaged in collecting knowledge and acting on it.

One seemingly minor way of protecting the common man is through patent protection laws, such as those that the US has. But patent protection is anything but inconsequential. Robertson gives a striking example comparing the USA with Mexico, and two of the richest men in the world, one in Mexico and one in the USA. Bill Gates became the world's richest man for a few years by creating a company, Microsoft, based on innovation that created many jobs and distributed wealth to many individuals. Microsoft could not have succeeded if it were not for its ability to copyright and patent its software and expect the federal government to enforce that protection. These things were provided by the US government. The other 'world's richest man'; was Mexican Carlos Slim. When Mexico privatized its national phone company, it gave Carlos Slim monopolistic control of the phone company. This funneled hundreds of billions of dollars into Carlos Slim's personal bank account. In other words, the Mexican government parceled out wealth, not based on merit, but based on personal connections. According to the OECD (2012), this reduced the GDP of Mexico by 2% a year from 2005 to 2009. This reduced income for the country by $130 billion. Why did Mexico do this?

The Mexican legal system is relatively weak, and the country has always been dominated by wealthy individuals. Modern Mexico, a nation of 130 million, formally became a nation in 1810. But it was initially set up as a colony of Spain 300 years earlier for the purpose of shipping wealth back to Iberia (Spain). The country was always dominated by wealthy 'patrons;' landowners with Spanish blood. So, the principles of equality and the protection of individual rights, especially for the indigenous people, were NOT there in the beginning. Subsequently, wealthy individuals have never been talked into setting up constitutional guarantees for the rights of individuals.

In contrast, when the US Constitution was being authored, the spirit of equality (between landed white males) prevailed. The laws were written to grant patent rights based solely on the merits of the inventions and could not be granted by men in positions of authority or power. The British had taken steps for hundreds of years in the direction of democracy, starting with the Magna Carta in 1215, which limited the powers of the king to use unbridled force to settle disputes with the barons of British fiefdoms.

It's also worth noting that Spanish colonies in the new world were all "extractive," to use James Robinson's (2012) terminology. The Spanish colonies existed solely to extract wealth from the colonies and ship it to Spain. As such, they had the notion of deferential privilege built into their very bones. The nations of Central and South America to this day are plagued by the legacy of inequality.

This is in stark contrast to the British colonies throughout the world. Luckily for these colonies, Great Britain had a tradition of democratic (somewhat distributed power-sharing) governance which they attempted to bring to their colonies. Given this, one would expect the more democratic nations of Singapore, India, Canada, Australia, New Zealand, and a few other ex-

British colonies to outperform the resource-rich nations with hierarchical governments in Central and South America. The huge differences in the success of the US and Mexico can be traced back to the British spirit of distributing governing power, in contrast to the Spanish spirit of concentrating power in the hands of rulers. The fact that these effects linger on today is testimony to the difficulty in changing federal governments.

We see here yet another example of how distributing power increases the organizational intelligence, and therefore their chances of success, while concentrating power destroys it. If enough people were educated to understand the principles of collective and organizational intelligence, perhaps governments could be changed for the better.

9.8 National Decisions: Deliberative Polling

Organizational intelligence and certainly collective intelligence depend upon distributing information and then encouraging debate followed by decision-making mechanisms. Large democracies around the world seem to be gradually losing some of their effectiveness in combating social problems from an unlikely source: manipulated flaws in voting systems. In almost all democratic countries, people in power are manipulating which candidates get to run for office and even manipulating how people's votes get counted.

Stanford professor James Fishkin has an answer in his work, Democracy and Deliberation: New Directions for Democratic Reform (1991). He suggests selecting a representative sample from within the nation, which may have many millions of people, and have this representative sample of people get together to discuss issues face-to-face. A representative sampling means that most of the viewpoints that people care about in different communities across the land are represented in the people that are included in the sample. For most nations, the representative sample should probably have a few hundred people. This is still too large to have good discussions. These large groups need to be decomposed into discussion groups with diverse membership that are moderated, let's say of approximately 15 individuals per group. Note the words diverse and moderated.

In Chapter 2, when we talked about cultivating collective intelligence, it was emphasized that diversity makes groups more intelligent, and that moderated discussions are absolutely essential. According to the science of intelligent decision-making, every person in a group must have their time to speak, no one can dominate, and no one can criticize. In Fishkin's (1991) model, smaller groups – after having been informed about an issue by trained, balanced presenters - would debate amongst themselves, and then publicly announce the most important ideas they had developed. Thereafter, the full assembly would be exposed to the ideas.

Prof. Fishkin said, in 2018, that he had used his technique, which is a variation of this one, on 28 nations and 109 different events to hammer out political decisions.

According to *Wikipedia,* the representatives start out their weekend deliberations with briefing materials which are made from input from all interested parties before they arrive. Emotion is stripped away and only facts are presented. The people are asked to register their considered opinions after a day or more of group discussions, i.e., deliberation. They vote at the end of their deliberations. It was used in 2017 in South Korea to decide what to do with two nuclear power plants that were almost completed when the Fukushima nuclear power plants had their meltdown in Japan (Fishkin, 2018). There were strongly held divergent views in the public and in the government – and in the microcosms before being informed and deliberated. But after the deliberative discussions and polling orchestrated by Prof. Fishkin, they all agreed on a compromise in which the two power plants would be completed, but no further ones would be funded.

Another successful conclusion was accomplished in emotion-laden Texas on the question of wind power versus oil. As you know, Texas is oil country, and putting wind generating towers across the landscape did not appeal to many folks at the beginning. After their deliberative discussions and polling, Texas decided to start using wind energy in a big way appropriate to Texas, i.e., they went from being last in the nation to being first in the nation in the production and consumption of wind-generated electricity.

As of 2020, deliberative polls have taken place around the world, including in Argentina, Canada, Brazil, the United States, Ghana, Tanzania, Uganda, China, Hong Kong, Japan, Korea, Bulgaria, Denmark, Greece, Hungary, Italy, Northern Ireland, Poland, Croatia, the United Kingdom, the European Union, and Australia – and is a part of governance in Mongolia.

Deliberative decision-making should be practiced in companies as well as nations since it increases the collective intelligence of the organizations involved.

9.9 Final Five Ranked Voting

Gathering representative information and discussing it still leaves open the question of final decision-making. Do you give everyone a 'single vote' on a particular issue?

There is another mechanism beyond voting for intelligent decision-making in teams, groups and even nations. It's called final five ranked voting and has been proposed by Katherine Gehl and Michael E. Porter. It is described by Gehl in her TED talk "US politics isn't broken. It's fixed." (2020). It fixes some of the flaws in the voting system currently used in the USA.

It works by starting with an open-to-anyone primary. This is followed by a selection of the top five candidates based on the popular vote. This is followed, at a later date, by instant runoffs among the top five using ranked-choice voting. In the second stage, instead of going for only one of the five individuals, voters rank-order their preferences for all five candidates. Out of the five candidates, the one who received the least votes is dropped, and the second ranked candidates of those who had voted for this candidate are distributed. Out of the four remaining candidates, the one who received the least number of votes is dropped, and so on., until there is only one candidate left; they are then declared the winner. The candidate standing up on the final ballot doesn't need to belong to any party. This could break the stranglehold of parties on the legislative process.

9.10 Idea Market Voting

In the deliberative polling approach to deciding national issues, the final step is voting, and this is usually done by asking participants to choose the one idea they like the most. Another approach is to use the rank ordered voting scheme just discussed. But there is another solution, as well. This solution would give voters the right to vote on several ideas and register the strength of their convictions along with a favorable or negative vote. This is a version of the 'idea market' discussed in Chapter 3.

The ideas would be the issues that representatives brought to the conference for discussion. Everyone in the assembly would be given a fixed amount of fictitious money, e.g. $100. They would be told to invest their money in the ideas that they like the most, but they can never invest more than $200/N in any one idea, where N is a number of ideas under discussion.[9]

---

[9]If there are only 3 ideas in the market, the cap is removed, and participants can invest everything in one idea.

Suppose there are 10 ideas to choose from, and that the goal is to select the single best one. This would mean that an individual investor could put $50 on their favorite idea, another $30 on their second-choice idea, and $20 on their third choice. Then all ideas would be rank ordered according to the investments they received, and the bottom of the list would be trimmed, e.g., 3 of the 10 ideas would be eliminated. The state of affairs is then viewed by all participants, followed by short discussions in the groups of 10, and then investors' money is returned so they can vote again, and then investments are recast, rescored, and the lower investments are again trimmed, e.g., two of the remaining 7 ideas are removed. When there are only three ideas left to choose from, participants are free to invest all that they have however they choose, in one idea, or across all three ideas.

Notice that there is a great deal of similarity between this approach and rank order voting, except that voters can register the strength of their conviction for each idea, rather than a simple 0/1 (yes/no) vote for an idea. Allowing strength of conviction to be a factor makes this version of the idea market superior to straightforward rank order voting, and superior to asking participants to vote once for their top choice.

CHAPTER 10: THE RISE OF MACHINE INTELLIGENCE AND AUTOMATION

The evolution of intelligence on earth is a force of nature, like gravity. It exerts pressure to grow and expand wherever it can.

Modern-day civilization, in fact, is a result of the creep of intelligence into machinery. Nations that have more intelligent machinery have healthier citizens with longer lives. A thousand years ago, well before the Industrial Revolution, the average human lifespan was about 35 years. Now, in most industrialized countries the average lifespan is more than 80 years. And this gift of health and wealth was achieved by industrial machines and the wealth that they generated within nations and peoples.

The evolution of intelligence machinery is driven by the fact that machines can do more work with less human energy than human beings can do by themselves. It is also driven by the fact that machines could not exist without human social infrastructure. So, the evolution of machinery is linked to the evolution of the social groups that could take advantage of machinery, e.g., tribes, cities, and nations and ultimately the nations that make up civilization. Those tribes/nations/businesses with the most efficient machines survived because they had more wealth and power.

Machine intelligence itself is the result of compounded inventions and discoveries, each one building on the previous ones and encoding a bit of new intelligence. And this compounding of inventions and concomitant development of businesses and international trade has led to the development of artificial intelligence. AI is going to change our lives for the better more quickly and more dramatically than any previous development in history.

The field of AI developed slowly since its inception in the 1960s and then took an exponential growth spurt starting around 2015. The growth spurt happened for three reasons 1. The invention of deep learning algorithms and 2. massive amounts of training data and 3. faster, special purpose computers.

Deep learning algorithms are a way of training multilayer artificial neural nets. It was conceived by Geoffrey Hinton in 2004, and embellished by Yoshua Bengio and Yann LeCun, for which the three received the Turing award in 2018. The algorithms reduce the amount of training data required per layer in a multilayered neural net. This means that it is practical to train more layers, which in turn means that the overall power of the artificial neural net is increased. Using deep learning, it has become possible for the first time to train neural nets to drive cars, control robots, recognize speech and make medical diagnoses. And this has barely scratched the surface of what neural nets can do. But what they can do theoretically cannot become reality without data. None of the powers of neural nets would be possible with deep learning algorithms alone. Neural nets exhibiting intelligence became possible only when massive amounts of training data became available that could be used in conjunction with the deep learning algorithms.

Massive amounts of training data is a new thing. It just became available thanks to the general increase of the flow of digital data in the modern world. Ultimately, the data from the plethora of microprocessors in everything (especially sensors and mobile phones), connected by radio and infrared communication links to the internet, and storing digital data in the cloud, in addition to multitude of local storage devices (everybody's computer and mobile phone contains massive amounts of memory).

So, AI is not simply the product of individual computers getting smarter with high-powered AI programs, but rather the product of the global ecosystem of hundreds of billions of microprocessors supplying data to make machines smarter. And all this is coupled to the evolution of the global trading system where mass-produced items can be shared broadly. So, AI is more accurately described as being a visible part of the distributed intelligence embedded in all the microprocessors around the globe and the global trade infrastructure that ultimately finances is development.

To make this more concrete, consider some of the different parts ecosystem that GPS satellites make possible. One aspect is that self-driving cars are now possible using GPS. Another aspect is the satellite imaging of earthbound landscapes that is, in turn, motivating digital image storage which is, in turn, helping doctors with medical diagnoses using AI processing of medical images. It includes the mobile phone tracking that makes the detection of congestion on the roads possible. In addition to all the data being generated this way, consider that the social media, email, YouTube videos and all the other digital transmissions that surround us that are providing the data to make AI even smarter. All these things start with microprocessors, and they end up supplying the data to make AI smarter.

In other words, poetically stated, AI is a particularly visible part of global intelligence. It is made possible by the digitization of the world we live in, because that is providing the massive amounts of training data needed to make AI systems 'real world' intelligent. (Computer programs playing GO, chess, checkers, or similar games are not "real world" smart because they can train themselves against a set of rules, not real-world data.)

Another way of noticing the creep of intelligence into our machines is to notice that automation involves increasing the level of intelligence of machines. And automation is unstoppable. Automated machines have made it possible to sustain larger populations, which in turn has promoted even more automation. The economies of scale of serving large populations are actually economies derived from automation. The bigger the market, the more automation is possible.

Another factor promoting automation is the sheer size of companies. According to *The Economist*, Special Report on Companies, September 17, 2016, big firms are getting bigger: the number of publicly listed companies in America fell because of mergers and acquisitions by nearly 50% in the first two decades of the 21st century. Furthermore, big businesses which have $1 billion valuations or more account for nearly 60% of total global revenues and 65% of market capitalization. American corporate profits are higher than they have ever been dating back to 1929. Cash in big firms is piling up. They have cash equal to 10% of the GDP in America as much as 50% in Japan.

All this progress is accelerating toward an endgame in which automated machinery will be able to make everything physical that humanity needs. And machines will indeed be able to take care of humanity's needs, unless human greed, competition, and social problems thwart this outcome. Unfortunately, human greed, competition, and lack of empathy are all around us. Huge wealth disparities are showing up in the wealthiest nations as indicated by high Gini coefficients, e.g., the USA and Singapore. The Gini coefficient is increasing because wealth producing machines require fewer laborers while concomitantly producing more wealth for company shareholders.

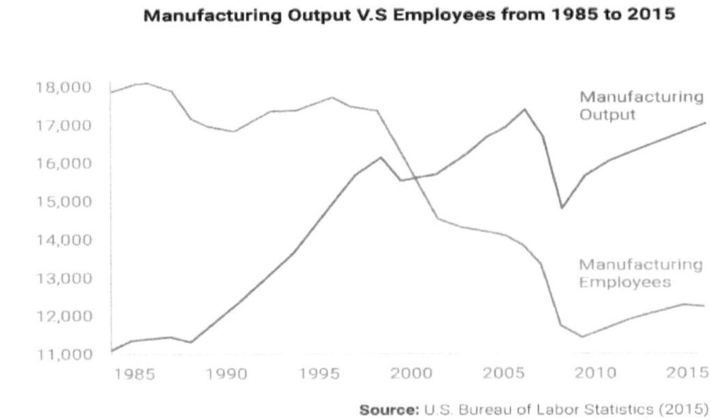

Figure 19: *Manufacturing Output V.S Employees from 1985 to 2015*
Source: ***U.S Bureau of Labor Statistics (2015)***

This graph shows how US manufacturing output is increasing dramatically while the number of employees in manufacturing is decreasing even more dramatically. These changes are being driven by automation, the use of robots, and AI.

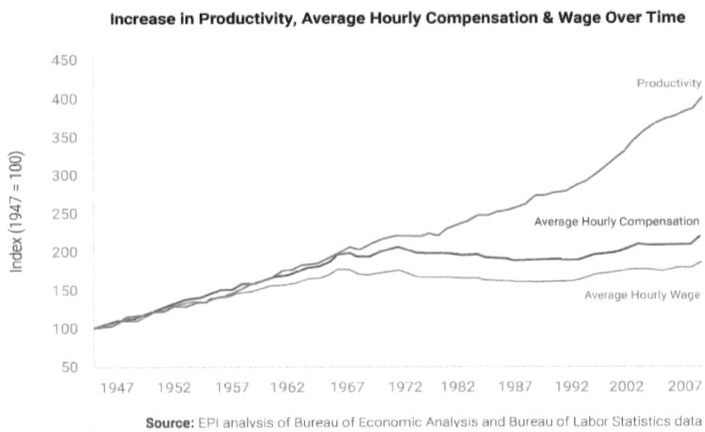

Figure 20: *Increase in Productivity, Average Hourly Compensation & Wage Over Time*
Source: ***Economic Policy Institute (2011)***

Unequal wealth distribution was not anticipated in most countries. The current laws in most democracies permit small numbers of individuals to be the majority shareholders in companies using automation to produce wealth. The machines make the shareholders very rich. (As mentioned earlier, the combined wealth of the 24 richest people on earth matches the combined wealth of half of the less wealthy people, 3.8 billion people.)

The 2009 book *The Spirit Level*, by Richard Wilkinson and Kate Pickett, shows that inequality in income reduces the average life expectancy and happiness in nations. Wealth inequality also introduces a host of other social problems such as drug abuse, teenage pregnancies, mental illness, depression, and homelessness. Wilkinson's book shows that people tend to be happier in nations with greater equality.

The fact that automation is accelerating gives its adoption an exponential growth curve. This means that the wealth gap between rich and poor nations is increasing. In other words, the more advanced economies are becoming automated more quickly than less industrialized nations, and thus the wealth of rich nations is growing more quickly than the wealth of poor nations.

This is the nature of exponential growth. But it has the undesirable side effect of exacerbating the wealth disparities between nations. Bill Gates said in his 2007 Harvard commencement address, "Humanity's greatest advances are not in its discoveries—but in how those discoveries are applied to reduce inequity." (2007). The truth is that Western economies are not doing a good job at reducing inequality at all. It would seem that our greatest ***challenge*** is not discovering how to produce more wealth—but in discovering how to distribute it to reduce inequality.

It would seem that companies that are first to automate will be the winners in the eternal competition for customers, because they can offer lower prices. As an example, consider Walmart, which is the world's largest retail merchandiser and world's largest employer (employing 2.5 million people). They grew to their huge size in 50 years by beating out the competition (Kmart, Sears, Woolco, A&P) by automating their supply chain more effectively than their competitors. When A&P, Woolco, Sears, and Kmart were driven into bankruptcy by Walmart, it was because Walmart did a better job of automating their business, and especially their supply chain.

The underlying reason for Walmart's success is that it had superior organizational intelligence. Captains of industry need to look beyond automation and ask if the information gathering and power dissemination mechanisms and their organizations would permit the kind of organizational intelligence that Walmart developed.

Netflix is a good example of a firm that avoided being disrupted by new technology. It started business by sending movie CDs to customers. But it anticipated that it would be possible to send movies over the internet - thereby reducing costs while increasing customer satisfaction - and it transitioned out of the CD market. Netflix demonstrated good use of organizational intelligence in forecasting.

The new kid on the block, Amazon, is eating into Walmart's business. Amazon is benefiting from more extensive automation than Walmart. Amazon is automating the entire shopping process. This strategic positioning will make it hard for Walmart to compete, but Walmart's culture of learning may allow them to adapt.

Often automation takes an entirely different technology path rather than simply refining an existing one. For example, when Netflix drove Blockbuster out of business it was by automating the delivery of movies using the internet instead of CDs and tapes. And when Japanese camera companies drove Kodak out of business it was by using digital photography to replace film. Ironically, digital photography was invented at Kodak, but they were unable to unwind their legacy systems fast enough. Storing images digitally is simply cheaper. The point is that automation can adopt intelligent machinery from seemingly unrelated areas to achieve cost reductions.

One of the most important points of this book is that organizational intelligence can be employed by companies to avoid technology disruption or mitigate its impact. In other words, if companies distribute information broadly, encourage corporate wide discussions, listen to input from employees, and have happy and optimistic employees who feel respected, companies can make better strategic decisions and are more likely to avoid disruption altogether.

Clayton Christensen in his brilliant book *The Innovator's Dilemma,* explained that 'disruptive technology' was the use of a novel technology in combination with a low market entry point that kept it below the radar of incumbents that would ultimately be disrupted (1997).

In other words, the incumbents don't notice the novel technology being refined by a non-competitor in a different market. They don't notice it until it is too late to catch up when the other company becomes a competitor. But we can be more precise. It's not simply novel technologies, it's specifically novel technologies that enable more efficient automation, i.e., it is automation that reduces costs that are causing disruption.

Christensen did not explicitly talk about automation, but the disruptive technologies he describes are those that turnout to reduce the amount of manpower required to deliver a service or product. This is, by definition, automation. (Sometimes the cost reduction can come from a supplier that uses automation.) However, the deeper problem that Christensen was tackling is why don't incumbents do a better job of avoiding disruption. Christensen's answer focuses on technology. But the problem is not simply a matter of technology. It is more likely inadequate organizational intelligence in corporate governance. When Schumpeter talked about "creative destruction" (1942) he was saying new companies are driving older companies out of business, and that's good for society because the new companies can deliver products and / or services at lower costs. This is just another way of saying that new companies are using automation more effectively than incumbents.

If the tools of organizational intelligence were to be used, the rate of creative destruction would probably decline, and the quality of life for employees in the incumbent companies would improve. Bill Gross of Idea Lab, and a TED Talk speaker, listed factors critical to entrepreneurial business success:

1. The idea,
2. Financing,
3. Management team,
4. Market timing, and
5. Business model.

He concluded that "market timing" was the most important factor on this list (2015).

Market timing is simply another way of saying a product or service introduction needs to coincide with emergence of enabling technologies which need to be sufficiently widespread to be the platform for the new business. Smart mobile phones provided platforms for apps (WhatsApp, Snapchat, Twitter, Waze) and the apps became platforms for new business opportunities. For example, Airbnb used the efficiencies afforded by emerging mobile phone / internet developments to automate advertising, reservations, billing, and recommendations. Traditional hoteliers couldn't compete being saddled with the inefficiencies of their legacy systems. Uber was another beneficiary of the ascendancy of the mobile phone platform, which enabled customers to use it for automated billing, connecting passengers with drivers, and providing driving directions. Cab drivers couldn't compete with the automated efficiencies of mobile phone / internet technology. The same is true for India's largest hotel chain OYO which was started just a few years ago by a 20-year-old using the same mobile phone technology used by Uber. The efficiencies of mobile phone-aided checking in/checking out, finding directions, ordering hotel service, and making reservations made it impossible for traditional competitors to compete.

The point of these stories is not about mobile phone technology, it's about the efficiencies that come with automation.

Microsoft and Apple are both more than 50 years old. If they were like most other companies, they would be in decline. Most companies go through their peak between 5 and 15 years after their founding. Never before have we seen such a run-up in market capitalization in a mature company, and it's happening because they are supporting so much of the digital backbone of automation. The extraordinary market capitalization of Apple, Amazon, Alphabet/Google, Microsoft, and Facebook is explicitly because they are the leading suppliers of *digital tools for automation.*

Business leaders who understand the evolutionary pressures behind automation can do a better job of forecasting competitive threats as well as helping their companies develop the right products and services. As powerful as the economic forces are to automate, another force beyond making money must prevail as our companies make decisions to automate. It is the force of 'conscience.' We human beings intuitively know right from wrong. We know our companies must put a higher value on the health of the planet than we did in the past. Making machines more efficient by making them more intelligent does not give them human values. To create the world we want, we must not compromise on moral issues within our various organizations. We must practice the moral standards of the world we want to bequeath to our children as we build our little corner in the civilization of the future. We all must vote with our pocketbooks, our social media, and casual conversations. And we must get ethical & moral issues on the agenda of business meetings. By being visible and taking a position, we can influence the evolution of intelligence around us to better reflect human values.

The good news is that the evolution of organizational intelligence must listen to the needs of people because organizations need people. People are the creative engines in organizations. People are more creative and productive when they are happy, inspired, and well cared for. So, the rules of governance, 'the genes' of successful organizations must accommodate the needs of people. And if the stock market is any indication, those companies that are ethical, socially responsible, and care for the needs of their employees, are better investments than those companies that don't score so well in the aforementioned categories.

CHAPTER 11: CONCLUSION

11.1 The Theory

This book is about the evolution of intelligence in businesses and nations. These are constantly evolving, being driven by the same laws of nature that created life. As with organic lifeforms, businesses with higher intelligence survive longer and are more successful. What we see with the rise and fall of nations and companies is, in fact, the evolution of organizational intelligence, and it is increasing over time. Our world is becoming more intelligent.

By thinking of companies and nations as having intelligence, we have a broader set of tools to understand economic development and corporate success. Business theorists and economic forecasters often mention organizational genes, but they seldom go so far as to mention "intelligence" in framing their ideas. In fact, good organizational genes allow organizations to learn, adapt and respond to challenges and thus exhibit all the properties of intelligent behavior. Contemplating this dynamic should allow us to predict what businesses or nations are likely to succeed or fail, or in the best cases, achieve excellence.

The wealth of nations is generated by the business organizations operating within the infrastructure provided by governmental units (nations, states, counties, municipalities, and city councils). Their success depends on their 'genes' (rules and regulations, constitutions, laws, protocols, customs, and so on), and their ability to learn from experiences over time. Learning must be continual because the playing field is constantly changing in response to competitive pressures. Adaptation must be baked into the DNA of governments and businesses for them to survive long-term and to compete with new players in our evolving world.

Most of the chapters in this book are dedicated to examples of how organizational intelligence grows or declines depending on organizational genes that support collective intelligence and organizational learning. The examples given illustrate that organizational intelligence tends to decrease, on average, when human discretion is replaced with automation, rules and regulations, lack of trust, centralized planning, and directives from senior executives.

In contrast, organizational intelligence tends to *increase* the more information is disseminated, the more discussion takes place, and as the greater the use of the tools of collective intelligence: team diversity, equal participation in discussions, respect, civility, employee involvement in goal setting, employee happiness, optimism, opportunities for employee learning, teaming, social responsibility of the organization, vision, and so forth. All of these terms, and more, were discussed in Chapters 2 & 3. An explicit list was given in section 3.11 of Chapter 3.

These practices and attributes apply to governmental organizations as well as businesses and can be considered to be the good genes for organizational intelligence.

11.2 Practical Advice

Much practical advice can be gleaned from the seven examples given in Chapter 7 where we covered Semco, Walmart, IDEO, Google, Zappos, Zain, and Visa. Each of these companies had unique approaches to organizational intelligence and their key organizational "genes" were described.

Organizational intelligence is a dynamic phenomenon. It constantly learns. It grows and shrinks over time depending on feedback from the environment, as well as evolution of internal rules of governance which constantly change. In the case of business, learning opportunities come from suppliers, competitors, and customers (inside consumers of information as well as outside consumers of product/services). Learning by itself is useless and to make it useful, mechanisms must be provided so that information learned can impact operations and planning.

Planning must involve both strategic long-term survival issues as well as short-term operational details. Operational planning should not be done by a small number of senior executives but by the implementers. Implementers should be able to change plans dynamically supported with rich real-time feedback channels from consumers of whatever work they are performing. Planning for strategic long-term issues should involve specialists in strategy, typically the CEO, but this needs to be augmented with input from most, if not all, members of a company.

Care must be taken to be sure that information flows freely and decisions are made using collective intelligence techniques. Egotistical CEOs who exude self-confidence are usually operationally inferior to humble CEOs, because they don't use collective intelligence. The most effective CEOs are the ones who are best at mining the collective learning that is taking place in their companies, as was discussed in section 4.3 and 5.1.

A well-informed group operating with the rules of collective intelligence is always superior to a CEO making unilateral decisions, regardless of the experience or the pay of the CEO. The Board of Directors of companies should make it clear that the CEO is the spokesperson for company decisions, not a unilateral decision-maker.

It is desirable to have charismatic leaders (CEO/Pres.) to marshal support from investors, customers, citizens, and employees. However, leaders should not be defining a vision and then directing others to follow the vision. Rather they should be ambassadors evangelizing the results of the deliberative discussions of executive teams. CEOs should generally set the stage upon which executive teams perform, and refrain from meddling while they do their work.

Here are three more guiding principles for promoting the development of organizational intelligence, to augment the ones just given:

1. Distribute power broadly,
2. Promote information transparency and sharing,
3. Monitor new technologies and extrapolate consequences thereof.

Concerning 1, distribute power broadly: the idea is to push power away from central focal points and distribute it broadly to as many people as practical - thereby maximizing individual discretion and trust - and minimizing paperwork and scrutiny. The world's biggest financial organization (Visa International) came into existence and grew to its present huge size by emphasizing this principle and thereby sharing power equally between member banks.[10]

The principle of power dispersion explains why democracies generally do better than the various government that practice centralized decision-making. For example, consider the failures of mainland China 60 years ago (45 million people starved to death), North Korea (widespread starvation has been the norm for many years), and several Central American and South American nations in their experiments with centralized planning. These failures are in stark contrast to the successes of South Korea, the USA, and democratic European nations.

The one exception to decentralizing power is a national defense system. Defense systems require centralized planning and execution, and some

---

[10]Dee Hock, author of *The Birth of the Chaordic Age* and founder of Visa evangelized the idea that centralized control should be minimized, and companies should run as close to the boundary of chaos as possible.

planning must be done in secret. That said, much of the required planning need not be secret and better decisions can be made gathering information from all citizens who want to register an opinion.

Business democracies are also superior to the typical hierarchical authoritarian structure of most companies. Recall the stories in this book about Visa, Zappos, Semco, SRC Holdings, and so on. They all owe their remarkable successes to pushing power and autonomy into the hands of employees and trusting them to make good decisions whatever their job may be.

Concerning 2, promote information transparency and sharing: most information about most aspects of business should be freely available to anyone in the company. The flow of money, materials, work-in-process, or creative work should be visible to everyone, and efforts should be made to make such information easy to understand and constantly updated.

Standard operating procedure should include summarization and posting of information learned from outside or inside sources, so that everyone in the company who desires information can easily find it.

As a practical matter, the role of managers should be less about management and more about making sure subordinates can quickly find information. The goal is to inform everyone of factors that may impact their livelihood. This would usually include information about the competitive environment, customers / consumers, and the availability of resources. The best organizational structures make information available for ready access when people need it, not handed out periodically in meetings.

Concerning 3, monitoring new technologies and extrapolating consequences thereof: this is where companies implicitly determine their long-run fate, and whether or not they will have an opportunity to evolve to survive a technology disruption assault. Or alternatively, possibly ride the next technology wave and be a beneficiary of the next big thing.

This is clearly a hard thing to get right, given the demise of some many industrial giants in previous decades. For example, IBM was once the world's largest technology company and dominated the world of computer hardware and software. Strangely it made the decision to step aside and allow two startups, Apple and Microsoft, to become the world's largest corporations in hardware and software. This can't have been intentional. It probably would not have been the outcome had IBM employed collective intelligence to make their strategic decisions.

There isn't an easy answer to questions of how new technologies should be monitored, and how companies should respond as technology around them evolves. Most companies have R&D operations intended to protect against disruption and promote internal operations. But technology has many faces, it goes far beyond what can be encapsulated in an R&D lab. Technology issues must be integrated with business issues and social trends, at a minimum.

The reason technology is so important: Civilization is based on technology, and so are individual companies trying to survive evolving modern-day competition. But few companies understand the underlying direction of evolution of technology. The following paragraphs discuss the direction of evolution and should enable more accurate predictions by strategic planners.

Thousands of years ago we began creating tools that helped produce food, shelter, and clothing *using less energy than would have been required had the work been done with our bare hands.* As civilization took shape, these tools grew into machines, and these machines have, over time, increased in efficiency, *doing more work with less human energy.* The machines could not exist without human social infrastructure. So, the evolution of machinery is connected lockstep to the evolution of the social fabric of tribes, businesses, and national organizations, i.e., civilization. Those tribes/nations/businesses with the most efficient machines survived because they had more wealth and power. The process started out with machines grinding grains, then making cloth, steam engines, steel, and so on. The process of increasing efficiency has eventually evolved to include all the workings of business organizations including logistics, IT, robotics, transportation, communication, and so forth.

Efficiency, doing more work with less human energy, is the key. An increase in efficiency pays for itself, so inventors will keep making more efficient machines until fully autonomous machines emerge in all industrial sectors. This process has already produced microprocessors, computers, and AI systems which, when combined with the right machines, can do everything that humans do at lower costs than humans do it. It's important to pay attention to the phrase 'lower cost than humans do it'. It means that the endgame of this process is that people will not be needed for the production of wealth (at least not large numbers of people).

The efficiencies of automation are unstoppable. We are destined to live in a world of robots, and AI automated intelligent systems. Most people will eventually not need to be engaged in manual labor to produce food, shelter, or material possessions. We can already see the magnitude of this transition via the fact that a mere 24 people control as much wealth as the poorer half of the world's population. The rich get their wealth through ownership of the organizations that own the machines producing the wealth. Other results can be seen everywhere: the global economy is experiencing an explosion in efficiency driven by AI, robotics, and communication technology. This ultimately has to be good for humanity, but there are huge social and environmental problems along the way.

Mankind is beset with global threats unimaginable a generation ago: global weather catastrophes caused by global warming, global pandemics, widespread extinction of species, nuclear threats from renegade dictatorships, the emergence of global oligarchs controlling the wealth of humanity, the emergence of homeless and poor people in rich countries.

Confronted with all these issues, the *greatest tool we have for dealing with these* problems is organizational and collective intelligence. But to use these tools, large companies must step up to explicitly address the problems by funding the process of creating dedicated organizations, which would then engage in information discovery & prototyping, deliberative discussions using collective intelligence techniques, and then act determined by the results of deliberative discussions. Of course, I hope this happens, and I hope the techniques described in this book can help in some small way.

ACKNOWLEDGMENTS

I would like to acknowledge the insights and encouragement of Ted Kaehler, David A Taylor, Ph.D., David D. Thornburg, PhD, Arthur A. Boni, Ph.D., and Rick Cardin, PhD.

I would also like to thank my dear wife, who put up with my lack of social engagement while my head was off dreaming about the nature of the universe and the evolution of intelligence.

I would like to acknowledge and recommend three other books that I consider companions to this document: *The End of Management, Organizational Intelligence,* and *Superminds.*

For the first book, the full title is *The End of Management and the Rise of Organizational Democracy* by Kenneth Cloke and Joan Goldsmith. The title says it all: it is focused on business and advocates getting rid of hierarchical management and replacing it with something approximating industrial democracy.

The second book, *Organizational Intelligence,* by Gerald Cohen and Rado Ktorov, is all about information processing inside companies. The book considers 'intelligence' to be another name for information and how it is managed inside companies. It has very little to do with organizational intelligence as defined in this volume. But it does describe computational tools that would be useful in companies with organizational intelligence.

The third book, *Superminds,* by Tom Malone, dwells on the use of various information processing techniques and computer science-based tools to augment human group decision-making. It starts with the observation that groups can make better decisions than individuals. Augmenting collective intelligence could therefore lead to a 'super mind.' He then asks if we could augment groups with machines and the right software could we get even better decisions? The answer is clearly 'yes,' and his book explores ways of accomplishing this augmentation to produce super minds. Unfortunately, the techniques tested in the book did not produce breakthroughs, but they are baby steps in the right direction.

BIBLIOGRAPHY

Acemoglu, D., and Robinson, J. A. (2012). *Why Nations Fail.* London: Random House.

Achor, S. (Director). (2011). *The happy secret to better work* [Video file]. Retrieved August 18, 2020, from https://www.ted.com/talks/shawn_achor_the_happy_secret_to_better_work?language=en

Ackerman, B., & Fishkin, J. S. (2006, September 25). *Deliberation Day.* Retrieved December 21, 2021, from https://www.americanprogress.org/issues/general/news/2004/03/10/586/deliberation-day/

Al Barrak, (2015). *Opening Ceremony - The Second Entrepreneurship in Economic Development Forum 2015.* Interactive Business Network. YouTube. Available at: https://www.youtube.com/watch?v=fjELMtx24Bg&ab_channel=InteractiveBusinessNetwork

Amabile T., Fisher. C. M., Pillemer. J. (2014). *IDEO's Culture of Helping.* Harvard Business Review.

Aravena. A., (2014), *My architectural process? Bring the community into the process.* TEDTalks. Available at: https://www.ted.com/talks/alejandro_aravena_my_architectural_philosophy_bring_the_community_into_the_process?language=en

Bariso, J. (2018, August 21). *In 1 Short Sentence, Satya Nadella Summed Up What Makes Microsoft Different from Apple and Amazon.* Retrieved December 21, 2021, from https://www.inc.com/justin-bariso/in-1-short-sentence-satya-nadella-summed-up-what-makes-microsoft-different-from-apple-amazon.html

Blanchard, K. H., and Johnson, S. (1982). *The One Minute Manager.* New York: Morrow Avon.

Bloomberg Markets & Finance. (2020). *Thomas Piketty on Inequality, Trump, Wealth Redistribution.* YouTube. Available at: https://www.youtube.com/watch?v=9lySKu9MiOg&ab_channel=BloombergMarketsandFinance

Bock, L. (2011). *Passion, Not Perks.* Retrieved December 21, 2021, from https://www.thinkwithgoogle.com/marketing-resources/passion-not-perks

Bock L. (2015a). *How Google is reinventing the workplace.* CBS News. Available at: https://www.cbsnews.com/video/how-google-is-reinventing-the-workplace/#x

Bock L. (2015b). *Work Rules!: Insights from Inside Google That Will Transform How You Live and Lead.* Hachette Book Group. New York.

Callaway E. (2012), *Claim That Links Economic Success and Genetic Diversity Draws Criticism.* Scientific American. Available at: https://www.scientificamerican.com/article/claim-links-economic-success-genetic-diversity-draws-criticism/

Christensen, C. M. (1997). *The Innovator's Dilemma: When New Technologies Cause Great Firms to Fail.* Boston, MA: Harvard Business Review Press.

Christensen, C.M. (2001). *The Opportunity & Threats of Disruptive Technologies.* President and Fellows of Harvard College Coase, R. H. (1937). The Nature of the Firm. Economica, 4(16), 386-405. doi:10.1111/j.1468-0335.1937.tb00002.x

Cloke K., and Goldsmith J. (2002). *The End of Management and the Rise of Organizational Democracy.* New Jersey: Wiley Publishers.

Cohen G., and Krotov R. (2016). *Organizational Intelligence: How smart companies use information to become more competitive and profitable.* New York: Information Builders, Inc.

Collins, J. C. (2001). *Good to Great: Why Some Companies Make the Leap . . . and Others Don't.* London: Random House Business.

Collins, J. C., and Porras, J. I. (1994). *Built to Last: Successful Habits of Visionary Companies.* New York: HarperCollins.

Cook, G. (2017, June 20). You Do Not Think Alone. Retrieved August 09, 2020, from https://www.scientificamerican.com/article/you-do-not-think-alone/

Credit Suisse Research Institute, (2016), *The Credit Suisse Gender 3000: Women in Senior Management,* Zurich: Credit Suisse Group AG

Credit Suisse Research Institute. (2019). *The CS Gender 3000 in 2019: The Changing Face of Companies.* Zurich: Credit Suisse Group AG

Crowley R. (2015). *Conquerors,* London: Random House.

Davis. L., (2020). *A guide to collaborative leadership.* TEDTalks. Available at: https://www.ted.com/talks/lorna_davis_a_guide_to_collaborative_leadership?language=en

Duhigg C. (2016). *What Google Learned from Its Quest to Build the Perfect Team.* The New York Times Magazine

Eagle, N., Macy, M., and Claxton, R. (2010, May 21). Network Diversity and Economic Development. Retrieved December 21, 2021, from Credit Suisse Research Institute, (2016), *The Credit Suisse Gender 3000: Women in Senior Management,* Credit Suisse AG: Zurich https://science.sciencemag.org/content/328/5981/1029

Earth Science & Remote Sensing Unity, NASA Johnson Space Center. (2014). *New Space Station Photos Show North Korea at Night, Cloaked in Darkness.* National Geographic. Available at: https://www.nationalgeographic.com/pages/article/140226-north-korea-satellite-photos-darkness-energy

Eccles R., Ioannou I., Serafeim G., (2011), *The Impact of a Corporate Culture of Sustainability on Corporate Behavior and Performance.* Harvard Business Review. Available at: https://hipinvestordev.com/wp-content/uploads/HBS.report.pdf

Economic Policy Institute, (2011). *Hourly wage and compensation growth for production/non-supervisory workers and productivity 1947-2009.* Bureau of Economic Analysis. Available at: https://www.semanticscholar.org/paper/Financial-Literacy%3A-Neoliberalism%2C-the-Consumer-and-Arthur/7461858bc3630e7f94daa9b54c6edfd3fdd4e2a0#extracted

Economist. (2003). *When Small is Beautiful.* Available at: https://www.economist.com/finance-and-economics/2003/12/18/when-small-is-beautiful

Economist. (2016). *The rise of the superstars.* Special Report on Companies. Available at: https://www.economist.com/special-report/2016/09/15/the-rise-of-the-superstars

Edmondson. A., (2017). *How to turn a group of strangers into a team.* TEDTalks. Available at: https://www.ted.com/talks/amy_edmondson_how_to_turn_a_group_of_strangers_into_a_team?language=en

Finkelstein. S. (2003). *Why Smart Executives Fail.* London: Penguin Group

Finkelstein. S. (2012). *Seven Habits of Spectacularly Unsuccessful Executives,* Forbes Magazine. Available at: https://www.forbes.com/sites/ericjackson/2012/01/02/the-seven-habits-of-spectacularly-unsuccessful-executives/?sh=6540053e516b

Fishkin J. (1991). *Democracy and Deliberation: New Directions for Democratic Reform.* Yale: Yale University.

Fishkin J. (2018). *Democracy when the people are thinking.* TEDTalk. Available at: https://www.ted.com/talks/james_fishkin_democracy_when_the_people_are_thinking_how_to_revitalize_our_politics_through_deliberation

Foster, R. N., and Kaplan, S. (2001). *Creative Destruction: Why Companies That Are Built to Last Underperform the Market, And How to Successfully Transform Them.* New York: Currency/Doubleday.

Freiberg, K., and Freiberg, J. (1996). *Nuts! Southwest Airlines' Crazy Recipe for Business and Personal Success.* New York: Broadway Books.

Florida, R. (2001) *Technology and Tolerance: The Importance of Diversity to High-Technology Growth.* The Brookings Institution, from: https://www.brookings.edu/wp-content/uploads/2016/06/techtol.pdf

Florida, R. L. (2002). *The rise of the creative class: and how it's transforming work, leisure, community and everyday life.* New York, NY: Basic Books.

Fortune Magazine, (2015), *Women-led companies perform three times better than the S&P 500.* Available at: https://fortune.com/2015/03/03/women-led-companies-perform-three-times-better-than-the-sp-500/

Gates B. (2007). *Remarks of Bill Gates: Harvard Commencement 2007.* The Harvard Gazette. Available at: https://news.harvard.edu/gazette/story/2007/06/remarks-of-bill-gates-harvard-commencement-2007/

Gates, G., and Florida, R. (2016, July 28). Technology and Tolerance: Diversity and High-Tech Growth. Retrieved August 17, 2020, from https://www.brookings.edu/articles/technology-and-tolerance-diversity-and-high-tech-growth/

Gehl K. M. (2020). *US politics isn't broken. It's fixed.* TEDTalk. Available at: https://www.ted.com/talks/katherine_m_gehl_us_politics_isn_t_broken_it_s_fixed?language=en

Gildea, R. (1987). *Borders and Barricades:* Europe 1800-1914, Oxford: Clarendon Press.

Google, (2021). *How Google Search Works | Our Mission.* Available at: https://www.google.com/search/howsearchworks/mission/

Government of Singapore, (2021), *HDB About Us.* Available at: https://www.hdb.gov.sg/about-us

Gross, B. (Director). (2015). *The single biggest reason why start-ups succeed* [Video file]. Retrieved December 21, 2021, from https://www.ted.com/talks/bill_gross_the_single_biggest_reason_why_start_ups_succeed?language=en

Helliwell, J. F., Layard, R., Sachs, J., and Jan-Emmanuel De Neve, eds. 2021. *World Happiness Report 2021.* New York: Sustainable Development Solutions Network. Available at: https://worldhappiness.report/ed/2021/

Hill. L., (2014), *How to manage for collective creativity.* TEDTalks. Available at: https://www.ted.com/talks/linda_hill_how_to_manage_for_collective_creativity?language=en

Hock D. (2005). *One from Many: VISA and the Rise of Chaordic Organization.* San Francisco: Berrett-Koehler Publishers, Inc.

Hsieh, T. (2010). *Delivering Happiness: A path to profits, passion, and purpose.* New York: Grand Central Pub.

Hsieh T. (2011). *Core Values of Culture - Tony Hsieh* (Zappos). YouTube. Available at: https://www.youtube.com/watch?v=AbFIPc34AJ8&ab_channel=Entrepreneurship.org

Illinois Tool Works Inc. (2012). *ITW Forging the Tools for Excellence.* Fenwick Publishing Group Inc.

Kahneman, D. (2015). *Thinking, fast and slow.* New York: Farrar, Straus, and Giroux.

Kelley. R. (1998). *How to Be a Star at Work: 9 Breakthrough Strategies You Need to Succeed.* Three Rivers Press. New York.

Kennedy, P. M. (1987). *The Rise and Fall of the Great Powers.* London: William Collins.

Koen. P. (2014). *Prediction, Preference, and Idea Markets: How Corporations can Use the Wisdom of their Employees. Chapter 4.* Open Innovation: New Product Development Essentials from the PDMA. Available at: http://www.innovationresource.com/wp-content/uploads/2014/07/Pred-Pref-Idea-Mkts-112513.pdf

Levathes L. (1994). *When China Ruled the Seas-The Treasure Fleet of the Dragon Throne 1405-1433,* Oxford: Oxford University Press.

Lorenzo, R. (2017). *How diversity makes teams more innovative.* TEDTalks. Available at: https://www.ted.com/talks/rocio_lorenzo_how_diversity_makes_teams_more_innovative?language=en

Lorenzo R., Voigt N., Schetelig K., Zawadzki A., Welpe I., Brosi P., (2016). *The Mix That Matters: Innovation Through Diversity.* BCG. Available at: https://www.bcg.com/publications/2017/people-organization-leadership-talent-innovation-through-diversity-mix-that-matters

Malone, T. W. (2018). *Superminds: The Surprising Power of People and Computers Thinking Together.* New York: Little, Brown Spark.

Michie, R. (2017). *The City of London: Continuity and Change, 1850-1990,* London: Palgrave Macmillan.

Morningstar Inc. (2021). *MSFT (Microsoft Corp).* Available at: https://www.morningstar.com/indexes/spi/mstar/quote

Nadella. S. (2017). *Read Satya Nadella's letter to Microsoft staff after the events in Charlottesville.* Quartz. Available at: https://qz.com/1053788/satya-nadellas-message-to-microsoft-msft-after-the-attack-in-charlottesville-virginia/

Nadella. S. (2019). *Satya Nadella, CEO of Microsoft.* Stanford Graduate School of Business. YouTube. Available at: https://www.youtube.com/watch?v=rtgN27z0oi0&ab_channel=StanfordGraduateSchoolofBusiness

Nonaka, I. (2014, August 01). The Knowledge-Creating Company. Retrieved August 25, 2020, from https://hbr.org/2007/07/the-knowledge-creating-company

OECD. (2012). EAG2012 - *Country note - Mexico.* Available at: https://www.oecd.org/mexico/EAG2012%20-%20Country%20note%20-%20Mexico.pdf

Oxfam. (2016). *62 people own the same as half the world, reveals Oxfam Davos report.* Oxfam International. Available at: https://www.oxfam.org/en/press-releases/62-people-own-same-half-world-reveals-oxfam-davos-report

Pentland. A. (2012), *The New Science of Building Great Teams.* Harvard Business Review. Available at: https://hbr.org/2012/04/the-new-science-of-building-great-teams?referral=00060

Pentland. A., (2014), *Social Physics: How Social Networks Can Make Us Smarter,* Penguin Books: New York

Pentland A. (2018), *Human Interaction, Idea Flows, and Wealth Generation.* MIT Connection Science. Ed. 1. Available at: https://connection.mit.edu/sites/default/files/publication-pdfs/JOIM-insights-final.pdf

Pentland, A., Woolley, A., and Malone, T. W. (2015, July 15). The New Science of Building Great Teams. Retrieved July 01, 2020, from https://hbr.org/2012/04/the-new-science-of-building-great-teams

Peters, T. J., and Waterman, R. H. (1982). *In search of excellence.* London: Profile Books.

Piketty, T., and Goldhammer, A. (2013). *Capital in the Twenty-First Century.* Cambridge Massachusetts: The Belknap Press of Harvard University Press.

Piketty, T., and Goldhammer, A. (2019). *Capital and Ideology.* Cambridge, MA: The Belknap Press of Harvard University Press.

Pink D. (2009). *The puzzle of motivation.* TEDTalk. Available at: https://www.ted.com/talks/dan_pink_the_puzzle_of_motivation?language=en

Porath C. (2018). *Why being respectful to your coworkers is good for business.* TEDTalk. Available at: https://www.ted.com/talks/christine_porath_why_being_respectful_to_your_coworkers_is_good_for_business/footnotes

Pringle H. (2015). *How Europeans brought sickness to the New World.* Science Magazine. Available at: https://www.science.org/content/article/how-europeans-brought-sickness-new-world

Probst. G., and Raisch. S. (2005). *Organizational Crisis: The Logic of Failure.* Vol. 19, No. 1, The Academy of Management Executive (1993-2005), pp. 90-105.

PUHSD. (2021). *The Desert Survival Problem Expert Ranking & Rationale.* Available at: https://studylib.net/doc/9847005/the-desert-survival-problem-expert-ranking-and-rationale

Rock, D., and Grant, H. (2016). *Harvard business review: why diverse teams are smarter.* November 4, 2016

Rosenzweig, P. M. (2007). *The Halo Effect: . . . and the Eight Other Business Delusions That Deceive Managers.* New York: Free Press.

Rosling, H. (2009). *The best stats you've ever seen.* TEDTalk. Available at: https://www.ted.com/talks/hans_rosling_the_best_stats_you_ve_ever_seen

Sandberg. D. J., CFA, Quantamental Research. (2019). *When Women Lead, Firms Win.* S&P Global. Available at: https://www.spglobal.com/en/research-insights/featured/when-women-lead-firms-win

Semler, R. (1988). *Maverick: The Success Story Behind the World's Most Unusual Workplace.* New York: Berkley Sensation.

Senge P. (1990). *The Fifth Discipline.* London: Penguin Random House.

Shakespeare, W., Raffel, B., and Bloom, H. (2006). Julius Caesar, New Haven: Yale University Press

60minutes. (1989). *The 60 Minutes Interview: Herb Kelleher.* YouTube. Available at: https://www.youtube.com/watch?v=MyiI8FoJk54&ab_channel=60Minutes

Smith, A. (1988), *Fumbling the future: How Xerox invented, then ignored, the first personal computer.* Nebraska: toExcel

Stack. J. (2014). *Jack Stack on the Great Game of Business.* Speakers. com. Available at: https://www.youtube.com/watch?v=S0qw_GX8I5A&ab_channel=Speakers.com

Stack, J., and Burlingham, B. (1992). *The Great Game of Business: The Only Sensible Way to Run a Company.* London: Profile Books.

Stack J., Burlingham. B. (2002). *A Stake in the Outcome: Building a Culture of Ownership for the Long-Term Success of Your Business,* Random House Inc. New York.

Stack. J., Burlingham. B. (2013). *The Great Game of Business: The Only Sensible Way to Run a Company.* Random House Inc. New York.

Stiglitz, J. E. (2012). *The Price of Inequality: How Today's Divided Society Endangers Our Future.* New York: W.W. Norton.

Takeuchi. H., Nonaka I. (1991). *The Knowledge Creating Company.* Oxford: OUP.

Tapscott, D., and Williams, A. D. (2006). *Wikinomics: How Mass Collaboration Changes Everything.* New York: Portfolio.

theglobaleconomy.com. *(2020) GDP per capita - current dollars - country ranking.* Available at: https://www.theglobaleconomy.com/rankings/gdp_per_capita_current_dollars/

The Great Game of Business. (1990 - 2018). *The SRC Story.* Available at: https://www.greatgame.com/

The Little Book of IDEO. (n.d.). Retrieved December 21, 2021, from https://www.ideo.com/post/the-little-book-of-ideo

Thurston T., (2014). *Christensen Vs. Lepore: A Matter of Fact. TechCrunch.* Available at: https://techcrunch.com/2014/06/30/christensen-vs-lepore-a-matter-of-fact/#:~:text=Lepore%3A%20A%20Matter%20Of%20Fact,-Thomas%20Thurston%20Invalid&text=Christensen%20is%20a%20business%20school,can't%20predict%20the%20future

Toonkel J. (2015). *Insight - Does a happy employee make for a healthy stock price.* Reuters. Available at: https://www.reuters.com/article/investors-workers-sentiment/insight-does-a-happy-employee-make-for-a-healthy-stock-price-idINKBN0MZ0BA20150408

Ulukaya H. (2019). *The anti-CEO playbook.* TEDTalk. Available at: https://www.ted.com/talks/hamdi_ulukaya_the_anti_ceo_playbook?language=en

Walmart. (2014). *Sam Walton Receives Presidential Medal of Freedom.* YouTube. Available at: https://www.youtube.com/watch?v=WmZ7HxvQwpI&ab_channel=Walmart

Walmart Inc. (2021). *Sam's Rules for Building a Business.* The Walmart Museum. Available at: https://www.walmartmuseum.com/content/walmartmuseum/en_us/timeline/decades/1990/artifact/2636.html

Wilkinson R. G., and Pickett K. (2009). *The Spirit Level.* London: Penguin Books.

Woolley. A., (2013), *Collective Intelligence in Human Groups* (YouTube Video) Available at: https://www.youtube.com/watch?v=Bz1dDiW2mvM&t=79s&ab_channel=TepperCMU

Woolley, A., and Malone, T. (2011, June 01). *What makes a team smarter? More women.* Retrieved December 21, 2021, from https://www.researchgate.net/publication/51453001_What_makes_a_team_smarter_More_women

Wujec. T. (2013). *Got a wicked problem? First, tell me how you make toast.* TEDTalks. Available at: https://www.ted.com/talks/tom_wujec_got_a_wicked_problem_first_tell_me_how_you_make_toast?language=en

Wujec. T. (2010). *Build a tower, build a team.* TEDTalks. Available at: https://www.ted.com/talks/tom_wujec_build_a_tower_build_a_team?language=en

Zheng, H. (2020, August 16). Retrieved December 21, 2021, from https://en.wikipedia.org/wiki/Zheng_He

APPENDIX 1: STARTUP ORGANIZATIONAL INTELLIGENCE

A Business Constitution can lay the foundation for collective and organizational intelligence in a company, just as in a nation. The Constitution below sets forth principles that will improve a company's triple bottom line (revenue, environmental impact, and employee well-being) by creating the right culture for organizational intelligence to grow over time. It is a template which needs to be filled out by management and then circulated among all employees as they join the company. This is a distillation of Ricardo Semler's *Maverick* book, and *Work Rules* by Laszlo Bock, and this book. Following this template should help companies survive, be good for employees, good for investors, and good for the planet.

The template follows:

[The company name] affirms that our business exists for the benefit of our employees, the customers we serve, the planet we live on, and our shareholders.

1. The company Business Constitution is as follows.

   The company vision is ....
   (Long-term, 10 years or more, explained in one or two lines)

   The company mission is ....
   (Short-term, 5-year time horizon, explained in one or two lines)

   The company tactics are ...
   (What are the current activities and deliverables for the firm)

   The company's core expertise is....
   (What is the company uniquely good at).

2. Employee voice: The company will solicit suggestions from employees constantly and have quarterly public acknowledgment of suggestions on company practices of information sharing. Anonymity will be allowed at the submitter's request. The best suggestions will be shared with the Board of Directors.

3. Transparency: Every employee will be informed about how the organization makes money (or serves the community if the organization is not for profit). Furthermore, every employee will have access to company financials which will be written and explained simply so that everyone can easily understand them. Everyone will be consulted when budgets are being made, so that they know how much funding they might be responsible for. As far as possible, employees should have some discretion on how money is spent to accomplish the responsibilities.

4. Employee control and progress monitoring: every employee in the organization should receive a semiannual review (every six months). As part of that review employees will be asked to suggest new ideas about anything that might improve the company business or increase employee satisfaction. These suggestions will be anonymous but visible to all employees who can then comment on them. Those suggestions that gather the most favorable comments will be evaluated by committees for becoming part of the company processes.

5. Fair compensation: Employee's compensation - salary and stock options.

   Regarding salaries and bonuses -- Salaries will be expected to be close to industry standards for similar jobs outside the company. To ensure a sense of fairness among all employees, the difference in salary between the lowest paid individual and the highest paid individual will never be more than a reasonable factor, e.g. 20, regardless of job function, e.g. CEO versus janitor. Furthermore, no one in the company can receive compensation greater than 10 times the annual salary for the President of the United States.

   Regarding stock options: Stock options are encouraged and can be as large as five times the annual salary, but not more.

6. Disruption monitor: Employees are encouraged to help protect the company against disruptive technology threats from the outside. A significant the company budget is set aside to support employees who want to investigate and report on potential competitive threats. As for formal accounting such investigations can be treated as a standard operating cost, which would be in the same general category as the cost of insurance or R&D.

7. Promoting collision of ideas: As the company grows, it intends to facilitate communication events and channels that foster a sense of community. Special efforts should be made to maintain connections with about 100 people. Organizing people in these units may not necessarily correspond to functions of the business. Its purpose is to promote social interpersonal communication, and collisions of ideas.

8. Trust and respect: The company tries to minimize hierarchy. Managers work with subordinates to set objectives and then help achieve them. Performance reviews are accomplished by peer review. Employees will have some discretionary spending authority and be trusted to make spending decisions, allocate their time and resources to satisfy their objectives. Rules and regulations are generally replaced with statements of intent and objectives thus allowing employees to thus allowing employees to make decisions based on their knowledge of the company mission / vision and real-time flow of money and assets through the company operations.

9. Board meetings and all hands meetings: critical strategic decisions will be made by the Board after receiving votes on issues from everyone in the company. Votes will be weighted in proportion to the percentage of voting shares owned by employees and executives. Board meetings to discuss strategic issues will be held several times a year. The Agenda will be prepared by the CEO, based on requests from Board members, and suggestions from company rank-and-file. Whenever a Board Meeting is held, the company must hear directly from the CEO or President of the firm to explain to everyone in the company what transpired at the Board Meeting.

10. Standard operating procedure for making operational decisions and monitoring progress requires rank-and-file employee review of financial statements in meetings to be held at least monthly. In the group discussions, everyone present must be given an opportunity to present progress or problems. For matters of significance, everyone present must make anonymous votes.

11. Equity participation: In order to equitably distribute ownership and control, there will be two classes of stock: voting and equity participation. Voting shares in a company remain in the hands of founders and employees. Equity participation shares are the shares sold on public stock exchanges. Voting shares are redistributed over time to employees as well as founders according to levels

> of responsibility in the company. Thus, over several years' time, founders will have less control and decisions will be more broadly distributed among stakeholders home I see is clear. Board meetings will be held monthly or quarterly, and holders of voting shares and equity shares will be invited to participate.

Investors and company executives will have the responsibility to propose issues to be discussed in board meetings and will be invited to meetings to promote their proposals if they so choose. Ultimate decisions will be in the hands of shareholders owning voting shares which includes investors, management, and employees.

APPENDIX 2: THE DESERT SURVIVAL PROBLEM

The Desert Survival Problem

Expert Ranking Rationale

These two partial descriptions explain the basis for attaching numerical scores to each of the artifacts left on the plane after it crash.

1. **15 points: Cosmetic Mirror.** Of all the items, the mirror is absolutely essential. It is the most powerful tool among the artifacts for communicating your location. In direct sunlight, a small mirror can focus 5 to 7 million candlepower of light in an area that can be seen from miles away. In fact, the reflected light can be seen even beyond the horizon. If you had no other item, the mirror would give you a good chance of being spotted and picked up within 24 hours.

2. **8 points: 1 Pair of Sunglasses.** In the intense sunlight of the desert a form of snow blindness could be a serious problem by the second day......

The complete list is the sole property of PUHSD and cannot be reproduced here (see bibliography for link).

APPENDIX 3: THE B CORP DECLARATION OF INTERDEPENDENCE

This declaration is a noble vision which would increase the collective intelligence of the organization signing up to it.

Available at: https://bcorporation.net/about-b-corps

THE B CORP DECLARATION OF INTERDEPENDENCE

We envision a global economy that uses business as a force for good.

This economy is comprised of a new type of corporation - the B Corporation -
Which is purpose-driven and creates benefit for all stakeholders, not just shareholders.

As B Corporations and leaders of this emerging economy, we believe:

- That we must be the change we seek in the world.
- That all business ought to be conducted as if people and place mattered.
- That, through their products, practices, and profits, businesses should aspire to do no harm and benefit all.
- To do so requires that we act with the understanding that we are each dependent upon another and thus responsible for each other and future generations.

www.ingramcontent.com/pod-product-compliance
Ingram Content Group UK Ltd.
Pitfield, Milton Keynes, MK11 3LW, UK
UKHW041644031026
15587UKWH00001B/478

9 781871 891317